Alastair Hull and Nicholas Barnard

Living with Kilims

Photographs by James Merrell

With 266 illustrations, 180 in color

 Thames and Hudson

Frontispiece Balouch bag

Right Kurdish bag

Line drawings by Tony Foster

© 1988 Thames and Hudson Ltd. London

First published in paperback in the
United States of America in 1995 by
Thames and Hudson Inc., 500 Fifth Avenue,
New York, New York 10110

Library of Congress Catalog Card Number 94-62070
ISBN 0-500-27822-9

Printed and bound in China

Contents

Acknowledgments   6

Preface by Alastair Hull   7

Chapter One   **Origins and uses**   9

Chapter Two   **Structure and colour**   25

Materials · shearing and washing · carding · spinning · dyes · looms ·
tools · weaving techniques

Chapter Three   **Recognition and identification**   43

Forms, patterns and types   Motifs and symbolism · unusual forms
Characteristics of kilim-producing areas   Anatolia · The Caucasus ·
Persia · Afghanistan

Chapter Four   **Kilims on the floor**   89

Floor surfaces · kilim sizes · pattern and colour · durability ·
soft use · hard use

Chapter Five   **Kilims on the wall**   121

Hanging kilims · location and positioning · methods

Chapter Six   **Unusual uses**   145

Bags · a variety of shapes · decorative furnishings

Chapter Seven   **Collector's Guide to Sources and Services**   169

Collecting kilims · care and repair · further reading ·
international auction houses · dealers, importers and services ·
international kilim collections · kilims illustrated in the colour photographs

Index   191

Acknowledgments

The location photographs in this book were made possible by the generous hospitality and patience of the kilim owners concerned. Thank you.

In Spain, Michael Kane provided invaluable assistance. Marjorie Lawrence, Alayne Reesberg and Linda Miller made the New York shoots possible. We thank interior designers Mariette Gomez, Anne Korman and Stephanie Stokes for their help. Our guide in Los Angeles was Suad Cano, assisted by designers Cissie Cooper, Dewayne Youts, Sue Aldrich, Sandy Koepke, Mike Kreiss and Jack McSparin. Our work in Belgium was made a pleasure by Ann Keppens, ably assisted by Maggy Materne.

In the United Kingdom, Jose Luczyc-Wyhowska of the Kilim Warehouse provided excellent advice on Anatolian kilims and their origins, lending many examples for photographic purposes; David and Sara Bamford kindly helped with details on cleaning and repairing.

We thank the following kilim dealers and collectors for the use of their photographs:

Ann and Geert Keppens pp. 70 (Thrace, Bergama and Balikesir), 71 (Konya, *far right*), 73 (Malatya, *centre bottom*), 74 (Erzurum), 75 (Kars), 79 (Bakhtiari); Linda Miller p. 75 (Kuba); Clive Rogers pp. 71 (Mut), 74 (Sivas); Daphne Graham p. 76 (Senna, *centre top*); David Black pp. 72 (Obruk, *right*), 73 (Sivas/Malatya), 75 (Shirvan), 76 (Senna, *centre bottom*), 77 (Shahsavan saddle cover), 78 (Qashqai).

Acknowledgments and thanks are also due to the following for permission to reproduce photographs: Helmut Wietz, Common Film, Berlin (pp. 10, 13, 14); Hutchison Library (pp. 65, 66, 68 *below*, Photo André Singer; and p. 67); Gisela Horstkotte (p. 68 *above*); John Hillelson Agency (p. 69, Photo Roland Michaud).

And, finally, thanks to Tony Foster for preparing the line drawings.

Preface

by Alastair Hull

I FIRST encountered kilims in Afghanistan in the late 1960s, as one of the generation of young people who had the freedom to travel across Asia to India and the Far East before the closing of countries and borders, and the exclusion of visitors. Like many other Westerners, I felt an immediate attraction to Afghanistan, and loved the contrast between the harsh mountains, and the fiercely proud but kind people. I revisited Afghanistan many times in the years that followed, travelling over much of the country in ancient buses and brightly painted lorries. Many lifelong friends were made as I spent hours, sometimes days, sitting on the floor of dark and dusty little rooms talking about kilims and textiles to dealers and traders – all the while feeling textures, learning about weaving techniques and discovering origins. It took three years before I felt confident and knowledgeable enough to buy my first kilim, but thereafter I acquired an increasingly large collection which I bought in Central Asia and sold in Europe. Many favourites stayed on the walls and floors of my house – not necessarily the best antique pieces, but often those that told a story of a place, or a person, met during my travels.

Since that time I have travelled widely in Iran, Pakistan, Turkey and Syria, following the quest for kilims and their study, but my greatest affection remains with those from Afghanistan and Central Asia. The strength and simplicity of the patterns and colours reflect the closest ties with the traditional tribal weavings and with the character of the people involved. My own home is filled with these marvellous creations, and I hope that through this book many more people will discover the joy of *Living with Kilims*.

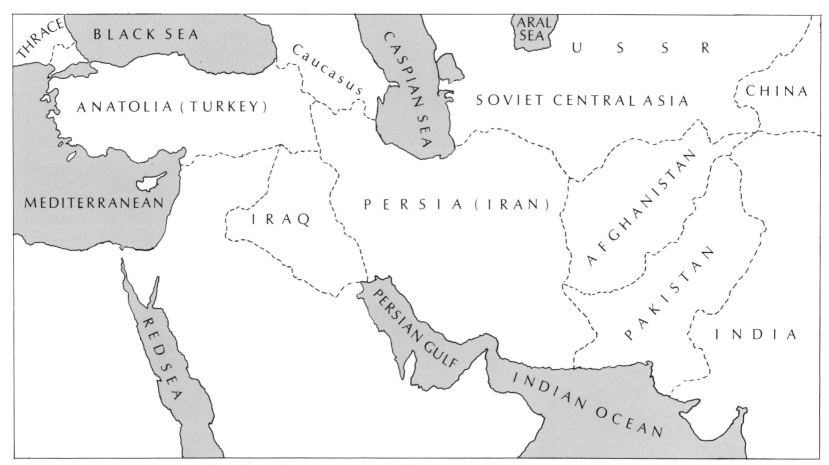

The kilim-producing areas from the Mediterranean to Central Asia

Chapter One Origins and uses

Origins and uses

WHAT ARE KILIMS? The word kilim simply means a flatwoven rug, or rug without a knotted pile. There are many variations used in different languages: gelim in Iran, kelim in Afghanistan, kylym in the Ukraine, palas in the Caucasus, bsath in Syria and Lebanon, chilim in Rumania and kilim again, in Turkey, Poland, Hungary and Serbia. Moreover, flatweaving is found in some form all over the world, from the Great Plains of North America to Scandinavia and Indonesia. At times there is only a structural similarity in what is produced, but the disciplines imposed by the materials and techniques often result in strikingly similar designs and compositions. *Living with Kilims* examines the flatweave production of the Islamic cultural areas to the east of the Mediterranean, principally Anatolia (Turkey), the Caucasus, Persia (Iran) and Afghanistan.

Until recently the kilim in general has been considered the poor relation of the Oriental knotted carpet by collectors and traders alike. For generations this view has prevailed, and the majority of books on rugs dismiss the kilim in a few sentences as an inferior and simple tribal product. In the last two decades, however, there has been an explosion of interest in the decorative, utilitarian and collectable qualities of these remarkable objects. Today, kilims captivate an ever-widening audience throughout the Western world.

Living with Kilims contains everything you need to make the best use of kilims, from their cultural and historical background to methods of manufacture and from recognition and identification to choosing, buying, valuing and repairing. Its focus is their use in interiors. Text and illustrations together show how kilims can enliven, enhance and blend into a wide variety of room styles, from postmodern apartments to historical and traditional houses, from a bright Mediterranean villa to a tranquil English country manor. The photographs are not of inaccessible museum pieces, but of everyday kilims that are readily available in the West through dealers, importers, merchants, stores and auction houses. They are kilims that can

Opposite Between 1873 and 1890, Ernst Holtzer – an expatriate German working for the Persian Telegraph Department in Isfahan – set out to photograph the traditional Persian lifestyle as the country went through the early stages of dramatic Western-influenced change. Here two women weave a kilim on a ground loom in a courtyard

still be used as they have been for centuries in Asia, as durable and decorative floor coverings, wall hangings and furnishings. All of them display the character and traditions of the people who have woven them by hand on basic looms, using weaving techniques, motifs, patterns and compositions that have evolved as they have been passed down from generation to generation.

The technique of flatweaving, the simple interlocking of strands of wool, hair or vegetable fibres, must have developed from the basic needs of the earliest civilizations for clothing, shelter and storage, and for simple comforts such as floor coverings and pillows. There are many historical references to weavers and woven cloth; the Iliad and works by later classical authors make it clear that weaving was an established and flourishing occupation of the time. Egyptian tomb paintings from the same period, and earlier, depict women weaving cloth and there are many biblical references to weavers and their tools. The domestication and selective breeding of the sheep, goat, camel and horse meant that wool and hair for weaving were readily available, and dyestuffs were synthesized from animal and vegetable sources. Production of the finest spun wool and dyes in the ancient world was sophisticated and international in character; fleeces from the Caucasus and dyestuffs from North Africa and India were traded throughout the Mediterranean and Asia, and the finished kilims were also important objects for trade and barter. Very few ancient flatweaves have survived to provide us with clues to the ancestry of the kilims woven over the last 250 years; animal hair and vegetable fibres rot and disintegrate over the centuries unless they are preserved in extraordinary circumstances. It is certain, however, that the kilim has been an essential piece of decorative, practical and portable furniture for the peoples of the Middle East and Asia for a very long time.

Kilims, together with jewelry, clothing, tent furnishings and animal trappings, helped to form the identity of the village or nomadic tribal group. Kilims were made for use on the floors and walls of tents, houses and mosques and as animal covers and bags; most were made for family and personal use, although some villages and towns of Persia and Anatolia became famous for their fine commercial production in the seventeenth and eighteenth centuries. Family wealth was stored up in kilims, knotted rugs, precious metals and animals and at times of famine or crisis any of these possessions could be bartered for grain, or be exchanged into local currency for use in the nearest market town.

Kilims have always played a central role in the family as part of the

dowry or bride price. Then, as now, the crucially important occasion of marriage involved much more than the union of two people. The girl, betrothed at an early age, became an instrument of liaison between families, to the mutual commercial, financial and political benefit of all parties concerned. The joint wealth of the two families was consolidated with rugs, jewelry and other items; the dowry also consisted of animals and grazing, water and irrigation rights. The young girl, learning alongside her mother and other members of her family, made her own dowry of kilims and textiles as a labour of love. Each piece embodies the inheritance of family traditions and tribal folklore. The position and status of a family were directly related to the quality and quantity of the bride's dowry, and this explains to some extent why the kilim has in the past had so much effort, craftsmanship and creativity lavished upon it with no prospect of financial gain from the marketplace or bazaar.

The ritual of marriage and the strictly conservative Islamic lifestyle of the nomads called for the handing down of traditional types of kilim, as this

Ernst Holtzer records an Armenian celebration, c. 1873–90; the kilim is from North Persia

13

dowry of two generations of a respectable north Afghanistan family – recorded by Parsons – testifies: 1 Purdah (woven curtain to divide the male and female parts of the tent), 1 Jaloor Paidar (tent door hanging, knotted or flatwoven), 3 Jaloors/Torbahs (door hangings and large bags), 2 pairs Juvals (the largest tent or camel bags), 2 Namak Donneh (salt bags), 2 pairs Kola-i-Cherga (tent-pole bags), 1 large carpet or kilim (11′ × 6′), 1 Namad (felt), 2 small kilims (6′ × 3′), 3 Parpak (tent bands).

These kilims were used in the traditional manner in the home, as floor coverings, cushions, storage bags, bedding covers and for ceremonial and welcoming purposes; the display of wealth was ostentatious, with valuable dowry kilims and textiles piled about the room, a veritable savings bank of weavings. This simple, pre-industrial, nomadic and village lifestyle has ensured an abundant supply of traditional kilims, with different tribes weaving their own distinctive designs that have evolved over many generations. But in the late nineteenth and early twentieth centuries, tribal groups began to lose their cohesion in the face of commercial and government pressures. Once tribes became sedentary and had to survive by trade and barter, they copied whichever designs were fashionable and saleable, and certain nomadic articles, such as storage bags, were no longer made. Marriages between tribes became more common, increasing the intermingling of often totally different cultures, and confusing the heritage of traditional arts. These changes were often accompanied by a decline in craftsmanship, but the fusion of clans and tribes of fundamentally different origins has sometimes resulted in exquisite and unusual kilims which have appeared on the market during the last thirty years.

Workshop production of kilims in villages usually indicates a nomadic tribe that has settled, in ancient or modern times, continuing to weave for domestic, and latterly for commercial reasons. In Turkey, for instance, kilims can be recognized by their tribe and area of origin to within a group of villages or even a single village. This compares with nomadic groups, who weave kilims within a much larger area, at their summer or winter quarters and sometimes at camps during a migration. The confusion of origins and names reigns supreme in Persia, where thousands of sedentary peoples from many different tribes have been forcibly relocated from one end of the country to the other in the course of its stormy history. The last such mass movement occurred as late as 1834, and one can imagine the chaos and tribal flux caused by it. The result is seen in the Persian kilims around Garmsar, for instance, which show a diversity and confusion in designs, patterns and colours.

Opposite A British officer, with his secretary and other soldiers, stands on a Caucasian Shirvan kilim. Photograph by Ernst Holtzer, c. 1873–90

15

Whatever the social and political upheavals, production of kilims continues unabated; but the traditional life of both the sedentary and nomadic tribespeople of Asia has come under a pincer-like attack since the 1950s. On one hand there is the attraction of the towns, on the other, the lure of profits to be made by producing kilims and textiles for the expanding European and North American markets. These factors, combined with the surge in tourism since the 1960s, have reduced the sources of original tribal kilims to a mere handful; only the least accessible areas are still weaving and dyeing in the traditional way. Afghanistan was, at least until the recent turmoil, the last reservoir of old and unusual kilims, and the major source of traditional kilim production.

By contrast, there can be no doubt that present-day Turkey has become the centre for the village and workshop production of kilims for export and trade; orders are placed by telex and many designs and colours are inspired by Western interior designers. Chemical dyes are used, and yet it is interesting to see the re-emergence of the rich, glowing colours of natural dyes, matched with ancient and often long-forgotten motifs and symbols, to satisfy an ever growing demand for more traditional kilims.

It is clear that the reasons for making kilims have changed greatly in recent years. Utility and religious and cultural significance have largely been replaced by profit and commerce. By looking at many different kilims, old and new, from many different areas, one can begin to appreciate those that seem to be original and not mass produced. These are the genuine article – kilims which retain their true ethnic identity, woven without compromise and with a craftsmanship that reflects love and heritage in their making.

Note: Wherever possible, historical and tribal placenames are used (e.g. Persia and Anatolia, not Iran and Turkey) with their closest equivalents in English spelling. Kilims have been woven since long before modern international boundaries were enforced, and many of the fiercely independent tribespeople are still hostile to repeated attempts to settle and confine them.

Opposite. A blaze of tribal colour and pattern leads the eye along this broad gallery at the top of a fourteenth-century manor house (see overleaf). The indigo, cream and terracotta shades of two magnificent Kurdish kilims are perfectly complemented by the mellow wooden beams, the collection of delicate seashells, and the plain, simple colours of the walls and carpets.

Every room of this beautifully restored home displays pictures, objets d'art, kilims and other textiles. An ancient stone fireplace and warm wooden panelling in the master bedroom are the perfect backdrop for a group of bold ethnic weavings, cleverly contrasted with dried flowers and antique lace. A huge Afghan kilim fills the oak-boarded floor from the foot of the bed (opposite) to the fender, where it is covered by a small Balouch meal cloth.

A profusion of textiles from Anatolia, Turkestan and Rajasthan fills the bedroom. Tiny mirrors glitter on a collection of purses hung between the windows, and a small Afghan kilim provides a soft texture beside the bed. A sunny window in the gallery (right) is curtained with a pair of kilims, held back with silk tasselled cords, and the polished wooden staircase (left), with its half-timbered walls, is the setting for a square Tartari rug and a superb old Senna kilim.

Floor space in the drawing room (opposite) is cleverly defined with a collection of small Islamic prayer rugs, their distinctive arch designs all pointing to Mecca. Colours glow in daylight from a garden door, and this scattering of kilims can be easily varied or moved, to brighten another room.

The mihrab of another prayer rug (above) leads to a small hallway where an alcove – guarded by stalwart stone lions – is defined by the elegant symmetry of candles and flowers arranged on an antique table covered by a richly patterned Bakhtiari kilim bag face.

20

In a SoHo loft apartment in Manhattan, comfortable seating is combined with tribal furniture in the conversation area of the living room. A Persian kilim, woven using the brocaded cicim technique, provides a central focus.

Kilims will enhance – and blend with – any environment. A spectacularly lit Anatolian prayer rug dominates the whole bedroom (below), complementing both tribal and modern art objects. Zig-zag diagonals across a large Garmsar kilim (far right) reflect the stepped line of a partition wall between the dining room and kitchen, and define a thoroughfare along the side of the eating area, well away from the scraping of chairs and unobstructed by heavy furniture. A narrow Anatolian kilim runs neatly along a passage, leading past the smooth curves of the loft's original classically styled iron pillars, and up to a twiggy modern equine sculpture, nosing an *Apache* bowl decorated with horse images (right).

Witty juxtaposition of ethnic art and postmodern features. The terracotta red of a north-west Persian rug warms the lime-washed maple units and cool, white walls of the kitchen, where an *African chockwe* figure holds a bowl aloft amongst the pots and pans.

Chapter Two **Structure and colour**

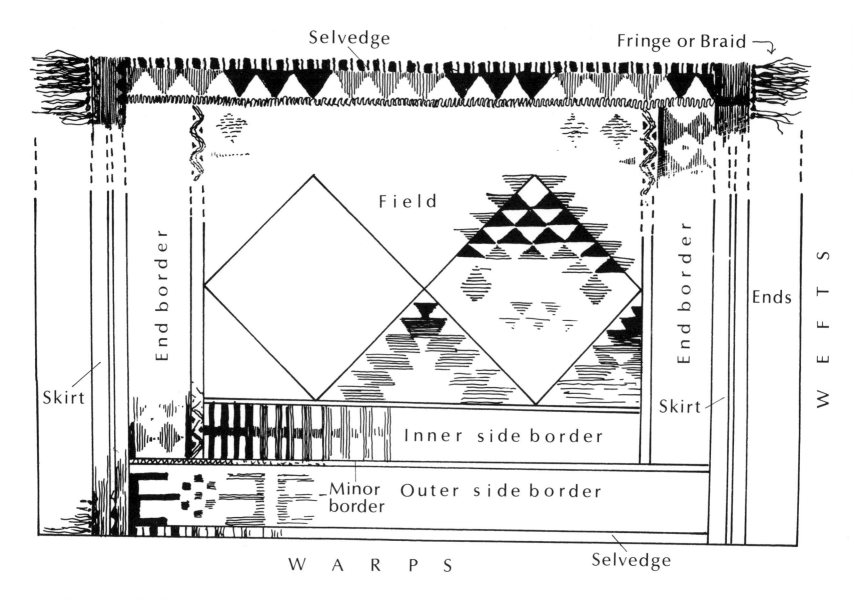

Selvedge

Fringe or Braid →

Field

End border

End border

Ends

Skirt

Skirt

WEFTS

Inner side border

Minor border

Outer side border

WARPS

Selvedge

The layout of a kilim

Structure and colour

In ISLAM an art object is understood without question as a blend of form, decoration and function in an integrated whole. The kilim is the perfect expression of this idea; the structure, pattern and purpose of a woven kilim, bag or saddle cover reflect the pastoral or nomadic lifestyle of the weaver perfectly.

Materials

Until the twentieth century many tribes were utterly self-sufficient in their weaving, a situation unknown in Europe since the Middle Ages. The source of the wool or animal hair, the streams to soak the fleeces, the plants and compounds for dyeing and the timber to make the frame for the loom were all found within their tribal boundaries, whether they were nomadic or semi-nomadic. Kilims from different geographical, and hence tribal, areas show startling variations in colour and texture, and this is in part due to the very specific localized sources of these basic raw materials.

Weaving is a craft of extraordinary antiquity. The weaving of blankets and mats using reeds and grasses can be charted back to the palaeolithic period and the use of animal wool or hair for weaving coincides with the domestication of sheep and goats, around 8000 BC. Throughout Central Asia the dominant source of yarn has always been the domesticated sheep, of which there are three types, fat-tailed, long-tailed and fat-rumped. The fat-tailed sheep are found throughout Asia and their tails can develop to an enormous size – 30 or 40 pounds has been noted. This pendulous tail not only sustains the sheep throughout the dry season but also forms a platter-like source of food for the pastoralists. The quality of wool from all sheep depends entirely on climate and pasture, and the wool from the fat-tailed sheep is famous for its hard, coarse and long staple that gives a lustrous shine with excellent dye-taking qualities. Up in the mountains of Asia, the cool, dry climate gives rise to a fleece that is much finer and silkier than that from the hot, dusty plains. No wonder that Jason sought the Golden

Fleece in the Caucasian mountains, home to fat-tailed sheep that have, in recent history, produced the very finest wool for some of the most technically complete kilims in existence.

Long-tailed sheep are found on the southern borders of Afghanistan and fat-rumped sheep in Turkestan, a tribal area that is now part of Soviet Central Asia. Unlike flocks in the more developed world, where breeding has produced fleeces of uniform colour, sheep are found throughout Asia which are brown, black, white and a misty red, all in one flock, and sometimes all on one animal.

Camels, goats and horses also provide a source for yarn. Goat hair is trimmed next to the skin, from beneath the unkempt fleece, and is used for its strength and its attractive, high sheen. The warps of saddle and donkey bags, animal covers and some of the kilims of Central Asia are made of goat hair, or of goat hair and sheep's wool combined. The sides of the kilims, the selvedges, are often of goat hair, and those made by the desert tribespeople of Balouchistan are frequently seen with fine goat hair stitching down the centre to join two narrow strips together as one rug. The tents of the Balouch people are made from a bent-wood, barrel-vaulted frame, wrapped in sewn strips of woven goat hair – a tough, if aromatic, structure.

There is a Persian proverb that says: 'The camel eats useless weeds, carries heavy burdens and does no one harm', to which should be added – 'and provides hair as fine as silk'. A better insulator than sheep's wool, camel hair is shorn from the neck, throat and chin, and plucked from the coat during the spring moult. Camel hair is used for both the weft and warp in kilims, to rich and subtle effect, especially when it is left undyed. This is typical of the older kilims of Persia and Afghanistan, although camel hair is still used today for twining ropes and bands.

Horse hair from the mane and tail is often tied in tassels on bags and, like goat hair, it gives added strength in binding and finishing a kilim. White cotton has always been used by certain tribes, and is becoming increasingly popular as a way of highlighting designs and patterns. Unlike white wool, cotton does not turn cream or ivory in colour with age. Its structural qualities are also much valued. Very fine kilims from Senna in north-west Persia, originally made for the court in a workshop environment, used cotton warps, as wool of an equivalent delicacy would have been very brittle. Since the turn of this century cotton has tended to replace wool in the warps of both Anatolian and Persian kilims. This is a good indication of how commercial zeal can influence traditional practice. Previously, there was no alternative to wool or local materials and a weaver would never have parted with cash for cotton to weave into a kilim that she was not intending to sell for profit. Cotton and wool mixtures are found in nineteenth-century kilims, and the spinning of the materials together results in a fine, strong yet supple yarn.

Silk is rarely woven into kilims and only the fine Safavid kilims of over two hundred years ago were woven in silk, interlaced with precious metals, for the fashions and ephemeral desires of the Persian court. Silk thread is used, however, as very fine brocade or decoration on storage bags of the Turkoman tribes of southern Central Asia, the Tekke and the Yomut. Precious metals and silks were coveted as the finest kilim decorations over many centuries, and it is amusing today to see their glitzy modern counterpart, lurex, in the most fluorescent colours, woven with pride into the contemporary, but traditionally functional, kilims of eastern Persia and west Afghanistan.

Shearing and washing

Shearing of the wool takes place once a year in spring or early summer, although in eastern Anatolia, around the shores of Lake Van, lambs are shorn in autumn, yielding a first fleece of short, weak wool. If possible, the washing of the wool begins before shearing, when animals are driven through a river or stream to remove superficial grime and debris. The fleece is shorn from the sheep with hand scissors or clippers, then washed, dried and washed again in a repeated process until the wool is clean. Soft water is ideal for cleansing the wool, and good streams and pools are jealously guarded by families over generations, their rights of use being an important part of the dowry exchange. The Qashqai of southern Persia scour their wool in a boiling solution of bicarbonate of soda or potash to remove excess natural fats and lanolin and in the Caucasus the fleece is pounded lightly with a thin board on stones to loosen the dirt. In the arid deserts of Balouchistan, eastern Persia and west Afghanistan the wool is left unwashed, merely shaken and exposed to the sun. In all cases, the cleaning and preparation of the fleece for spinning is complete after drying in the sun for a short time.

Carding

Cleaned wool and cotton is carded by drawing the fibres over and through pins set into a block of wood, or with the fingers alone. Throughout the Middle East and Asia an extraordinary technique has evolved at this stage for disentangling snags and clumps of cotton. After the debris has been drawn out of the cotton, a bow-like instrument is held over the fibres and

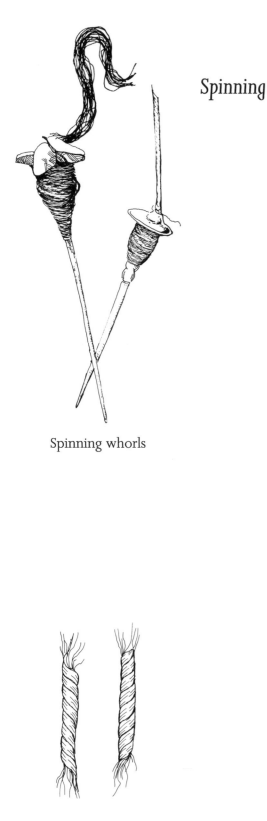

Spinning whorls

'S' and 'Z' twist in spun wool

plucked. The vibrations from this cause the fibres to become disentangled – an unusual, musical method of carding.

Spinning

Among the tribes of Persia, the nomadic Qashqai look down on spinning as 'women's work', but it is a very laborious and seemingly never-ending task. As with the harvesting of the fleeces, it is a family pastime and with training becomes an automatic task. Everyone in the tribe, male and female, young and old, whether watching over the sheep, engaged in lively conversation, or keeping an eye on the many children, will more often than not be spinning with small and light tools. The deft touch that rhythmically twirls the spindle twists the wool fibres together to create the yarn.

The very simplest spinning tools are used, from a stone weight, or a flat stick rotated horizontally, to various types of spindle. The drop spindle is a vertical wooden or metal shaft driven through a weight, known as a whorl. The whorl may take various shapes and forms according to family and tribal tradition – a notched disc, simple crossed splines, carved horn hooks, or a multiple notched square. Another form, the thigh spindle, is used by the Kirghiz, the Kurds around Lake Van in Anatolia and by the older members of the Balouch tribes. Here the spindle, with the whorl at the head or tail of the shaft, is rolled from thigh to knee or knee to thigh, depending on the direction of twist required. Throughout Afghanistan, the very much more complicated hand-turned spinning wheel is used, the spinning wheel itself being locally or family made using coarsely-carved wood and metal scrap.

From a bundle of fibres, or rove, held under the left arm, wrapped around the left forearm and wrist, or tucked into a capacious sleeve, fibres are teased out and knotted onto the spindle by the right hand, then suspended in the air by the left hand; the spindle is given a slight twist and allowed to hang, continuing to spin because of the weight of the whorl and the spinning motion imparted by the teasing out of the wool from the rove with the right thumb and forefinger. As long as the teasing movement continues and until it touches the ground, the spindle turns automatically, spinning and winding the wool into a strong, pliable and even thread. The lengthening yarn is then wound onto the spindle shaft, whorl or hooks and the process begins again.

The individual threads have a twist that corresponds to the direction in which the spindle has been spun, either clockwise in a 'Z' twist, or anti-clockwise in an 'S' twist. For right-handed people the natural turn is clockwise, and so most hand-spun yarn has a 'Z' twist. Two or more threads plied together give a very much stronger yarn. The direction of the spin of the plied wool is always opposite to that of the threads, so the plied yarn is balanced and less likely to untwist or break. The combinations possible at this stage are infinite, with plies of goat, camel and horse hair, metal, lurex, cotton and silk, with or without sheep's wool. Whatever the structure of the yarn, it is the process of hand spinning that gives so much character to the finished kilim. Hand-spun wool has a fairly loose twist with the fibres arranged nearly parallel to its length, and will give the surface of the kilim a smooth finish that soon acquires a supple sheen and lustre that enhance the colours used. Modern machine-spun wool, by contrast, is composed of fine, often frizzy and broken wool with intermeshed fibres that reflect the light less well.

Dyes

'The purest and most thoughtful minds are those that love colour the most.' John Ruskin could almost have been describing the weavers of the gloriously colourful kilims of nineteenth-century Anatolia and the Caucasus. It is colour and the way that colour is shaped by pattern that give kilims their abstract beauty. Throughout all pre-industrial cultures the art of dyeing yarn was an elevated and often highly secretive profession. Different regions and peoples became famous throughout the known world for their ingredients and dyes – the Phoenicians for their purple, the Indus valley for its reds and blues. Although we know exactly the ingredients used, the processes of manufacture are a mystery. Family and individual secrets were carried to the grave.

All natural dyes except indigo and some lichen and bark dyes, and all chemical dyes, need a mordant to penetrate the yarn and fix the colour. A term derived from the Latin *mordere* (to bite), the mordant attacks or bites the yarn so that the dye can take, and in so doing weakens the fibres to various degrees, depending on the type of mordant used. Yarn may be mordanted before, during or after the dyeing process, although the best results are achieved if it is mordanted *before* dyeing, and different mordants produce different colours from the same dyes. Mordants used in ancient times include compounds or solutions of wood ash, roots, urine, leaves and fruits. Today substances such as acetic acid, caustic soda, slaked lime, salt and the metallic salts of alum, chrome, iron and tin are used.

Until the mid-nineteenth century only coloured dyes from animal, vegetable and mineral sources were known and there were thriving industries associated with the cropping and mining of the raw materials throughout Asia. In towns and villages yarn would be taken to professional dyers, and naturally dyed yarn could be bought in the markets. All kilims made before the 1850s were, therefore, naturally dyed, a process that has continued until very recently. Nomadic or semi-nomadic peoples, making kilims for their own use, sometimes had access to natural dyestuffs – substances that grew wild amongst their grazing animals – and so the women would collect herbs, flowers and roots for their own special colour recipes. The migratory life only allowed for the carriage of small quantities of dyed wool, made up a batch at a time, and this is one explanation for the natural variations in colour found in the older kilims. People in desert areas, like the Balouch, were often unable to obtain dyestuffs from their barren environment and could not afford the pigments from traders and tinkers. Instead, they displayed an acute feeling for natural wool and hair colours. The Balouch are still the masters of this art, using camel hair that ranges from white and light yellow to dark brown, with sheep's wool in ivory and brown. Black and grey goat hair completes this subtle palette.

One of the oldest known dyes is a deep blue from the leaves of the delicate indigo shrub, recorded in use as early as the third millennium BC. Indigo is a native plant of southern Asia and was traded throughout Asia in great quantities in powdered form. The crushed leaves are soaked overnight or the powder dissolved in water to release a colourless agent. The yarn is dipped into this dye bath to soak, and as it is withdrawn from the vat, the colour develops on contact with the air. Each dipping, or a lengthy soak, will produce a darker colour and in this way every shade from sky-blue, through mid-blue, to almost black may be obtained. Indigo blue is pure and fast, resistant to sun, washing, acids and alkalines; but it is susceptible to friction as the less exposed or oxidized central fibres are revealed.

Madder root is the most common natural source of red dyes, and is known to have been in use in the Indus valley over 4500 years ago. Madder is a wild perennial, found from Asia Minor to China, with a deeply penetrating root structure; these roots are peeled before being ground into a powder ready for the dye bath. The intensity of the madder red varies with the age of the plant, from a terracotta red from three-year-old roots, to a deep purple at seven years. The mordants used must include a metallic salt and an alkali before the dye will bite and the final colour will also depend on the mix of mordants. Alum yields a red to orange shade, whereas iron gives a range of colours from violet to lemon yellow. Madder root dyes are light-fast and resistant to friction and alkalis but not to acids.

A whole spectrum of natural colours can be obtained from the flowers, fruit, vegetables and insects – even the earth – in the kilim-producing areas. The following list gives a good idea of the sheer range of materials used, and of the ingenuity of the dyers and weavers:

Reds Madder root, poppy, cherry and pomegranate skins, the bark of rhamnus and jujuba trees, roots of roses, rhubarb and apricots, petals from tulips and various insects such as cochineal.

Blues Indigo and egg-plant (aubergine) skin.

Yellows Safflower petals and buds, lemon and pomegranate rinds, onion skin, saffron, turmeric and the flowers of yellow larkspur and sophora, fresh stems of artemisia, leaves of apricot, apple, willow and wild pistachio trees.

Orange Grass roots, bark of plum trees or madder-dyed yarn dipped into a boiled solution of pomegranate husks, or of poplar leaves, or willow leaves.

Greens Walnut and olive tree leaves, sweet violet, double dyeing of a yellow with indigo.

Browns and blacks Tea, tobacco, mud and volcanic mud, iron oxide, and leaves of wild pistachio trees or walnut bark in combination with ferrous sulphate.

All of these natural dyes (with the exception of yellow) retain their colours extraordinarily well, but they do begin to fade naturally after about fifty years and will run if not well fixed. The positive aspect of this is that a kilim will mellow beautifully over the years if traditionally made with natural dyes.

Chemical dyes were first developed in England, in the 1850s, by one W. H. Perkin, a chemist who synthesized a mauve aniline dye from a coal tar solution. He began a colour revolution – the laborious and relatively expensive task of producing colours by natural means was superseded. The immediate results of the use of these new dyes in kilims and carpets were a reduction in the cost of dyes for the weavers, and a certain amount of disapproval among kilim connoisseurs in the West. For the first time, the weavers had a complete and relatively easy choice of colours, free from the limitations, and the natural aesthetic integrity, of the natural sources available to them in their homelands. Vivid oranges and yellows that had been so difficult to fix in the past were now readily available and easier to use. The use of chemical dyes spread rapidly, spawning village industries and reaching even the least accessible and most self-sufficient weavers of all, the nomadic tribeswomen.

Kilims produced in the first flush of this new craze display a rather startling use of many different, not always harmonious colours, and until recently some chemical dyes, such as aniline and acid-based dyes, corroded the wool, faded quickly and would not withstand washing with detergents. But chemical dyes do not always result in clashing colour effects, or poor durability. In the last thirty years chrome-mordanted colours have been developed that are indistinguishable, when used well, from natural dyes. Ironically, it is in these same thirty years that the natural dye lobby among consumers and collectors in the West has met with some success. Classes of instruction in the art of natural dyeing and a price premium for kilims with vegetable dyes have ensured a contemporary revival in traditional techniques among the kilim producers of Anatolia.

Looms

The looms used throughout Asia for the making of kilims are extremely simple and yet, combined with the ancient skills of the weaver, they are an essential part of a process that results in the most intricately patterned and tightly structured flatweaves. There are two types of loom – the portable ground loom and the semi-permanent vertical loom used in towns and villages.

Nomads, such as the Balouch, Qashqai and some Kurds, use the ground loom because its simple structure allows it to be easily unpegged from the ground, rolled and packed on an animal for migration and re-erected at the summer or winter quarters. This movement of the loom – often while the weaving of a kilim is still in progress – and its horizontal structure, make it very difficult to maintain tension, so that many kilims produced on ground looms are slightly curved, or have naturally irregular edges. Large kilims may be made up on these portable looms by weaving either two matching halves that are sewn together lengthways, or a series of narrow tent-band like strips that may then be sewn together in horizontal bands.

Ground looms consist of two beams to which the warp threads are attached. The beams are pulled apart to keep the warps taut and held in place by large wooden pegs driven into the ground at each corner. Tension can be adjusted with additional pegs, ropes and twisting poles. A tripod arrangement straddles the loom, from which is suspended the harness stick or heddle rod. Alternate warps are tied to this stick with string heddles and, when raised, these provide the shed – the space between the warp threads. Another pole, the shed stick, is inserted between the free warps, to create the countershed. The raising and lowering of the heddle rod and the movement of the shed stick create the shed and countershed between the warps though which the weft (usually on a shuttle) may be passed. The weaver will sit on the finished part of the kilim and move the tripod ahead of her as she works.

In villages and towns the vertical, framed loom is used for everything from prayer mats to floor coverings over nine feet wide. The warp beams are located in slots hewn into wooden vertical posts. The tension of the warps is adjusted and maintained with tension wedges. Balls of prepared yarn hang across the face of the loom, ready for use, and the weaver or weavers sit on a raised bench. Very large kilims, or more than one kilim at a time, can be made on vertical looms with continuous warps. The finished kilim or kilims are therefore wound onto the lower warp beam with the work remaining at the same height.

The number of warps strung on a loom determines the width of the finished kilim, and the length is determined by the kind of loom used. The texture of a kilim is determined by the thickness of the warps and how closely they are placed, and by the nature of the wefts and how closely they are packed. Some of the kilims from Central Anatolia are loosely woven and blanket-like; the cotton and wool kilims from Senna in north-west Persia are very fine, whereas the bags of the Balouch are so tightly woven that it is difficult to penetrate the weave with a needle.

Horizontal ground loom. This type of loom is used by nomads for weaving kilims and textiles. It is usually crudely constructed and easily dismantled for transportation by camel to the next camp

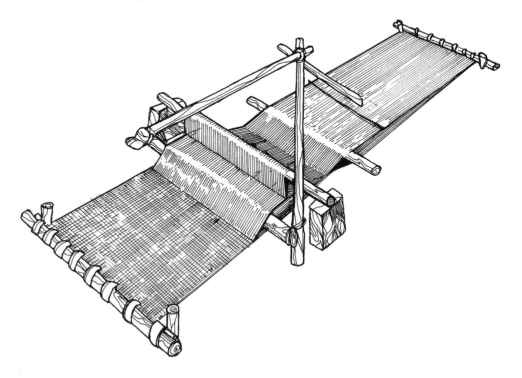

Once the loom is set up within the tent or house, or out in the open under a temporary canopy of old mats, blankets and branches, the weaving may begin. Traditionally, the weaving of kilims has been the preserve of women and girls, although where kilim production is an industry, as in Senna, men are often the weavers. Little girls begin to help their mother at the loom at about seven or eight years of age. Until recently a girl could be betrothed at five or six, and would have made at least three or four kilims to contribute to her own dowry. Not all tribeswomen were necessarily involved in weaving, and, as with all creative and utilitarian crafts, not all of the weavers were necessarily great craftswomen. The reputations of skilled and often elderly women weavers would spread far beyond the borders of their tribe and be converted to legend on their death. A young girl's bride price could be influenced by her skill as a weaver. Family patterns and individual designs would be passed down from mother to daughter, daughter to grand-daughter. The young girl might favour and improve a particular colour scheme or design, so that over the years traditional patterns would develop and be slowly modified.

Tools

Simple, home-made tools, such as combs and battens, are fashioned from wood and metal, and used to beat the wefts into place. The combs have very few teeth – usually less than five – and are sometimes carved and decorated with tribal symbols. The Balouch combs have very long teeth and handles which can be used as levers to force the wefts down very tightly.

Weaving techniques

A distinctive feature of kilim weaving is that individual colour sections are completed before the weaver moves on to other areas of the rug. This is in total contrast to knotted pile carpets, where the weaver works straight across the carpet in horizontal lines of knots, using many different colours in close succession. The kilim weaver will work on one block of colour, laying perhaps twenty wefts before beating them down with a comb and moving onto the adjacent colour.

Traditional nomadic weavers were unable to carry large quantities of prepared wool with them, and so would use whatever colour and texture of wool came to hand, each time the portable loom was set up. Because of this, the exact colours that the weaver had planned for the design could not always be found, and the kilim became an endlessly shifting colourscape, with details and idiosyncrasies that can be discovered and enjoyed throughout its life.

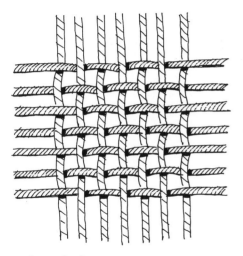

Balanced plainweave

Balanced plainweave This is the straightforward interlacing of the warp and weft on a loom. Where the warp and weft are of the same thickness, the result is balanced plainweave. The colour of both warp and weft threads will show on the surface of the kilim, so that they must both be the same colour for a plain cloth. The background for decorative devices, such as cicim and zilli (see below), is generally woven in this way.

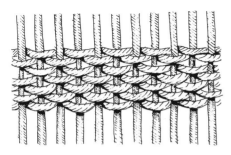

Weft-faced weave

Weft-faced or tapestry weave Here the wefts are beaten down onto each other so tightly that the warps are hidden. The colour of a kilim woven in this way is determined solely by the colour of the wefts, and the warps may therefore be monochrome or undyed. Such kilims will be either plain or decorated with simple horizontal bands of different colours. Weft-faced weave is commonly used for the ends of kilims, and of knotted carpets, as well as for tent cloths, bags and saddle bags.

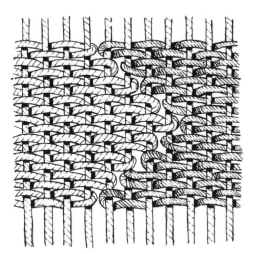

Slitweave

Slitweave This is the simplest technique by which blocks or areas of colour, rather than simple horizontal bands, may be introduced into the weave. One coloured weft returns around the last warp of its own colour area. The adjacent colour returns around the next warp, leaving a vertical slit between the boundaries of the two colours. Obviously this slit must not be too long or the kilim will be weak and easily torn. To avoid this the block of colour is stepped diagonally, which in the case of slits of up to half an inch long results in a bold geometric diagonal design of diamonds and triangles, or in a distinctive crenellated pattern. Sometimes the slits are very noticeable, but on very finely woven kilims, such as those from the Caucasus, they are often undetectable.

Many kilims are woven in this way, and most are fully reversible. Some kilims have diagonal lines of slitweave across a single colour area. These are known as 'lazy lines', enabling the weaver to work in stages on small parts of one colour section. When completing the rest of the section, the weaver meets up with the earlier work with a diagonal line of slit-weave steps, successfully breaking up large areas of one colour.

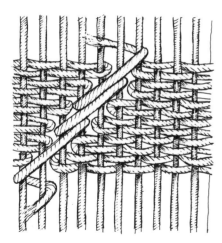

Contour bands

Contour bands There are a number of ways to cover or reinforce slits. Simple, contrasting contour bands can be woven between the blocks of colour, outlining each area, or, in a more complex method, the weaver can wrap extra wefts of a contrasting shade round pairs of warp threads between different colour areas. This produces a contour on the face of the finished weave, which looks as if it has been worked in after the piece has been taken off the loom. In fact the wrapping is done progressively throughout the weaving of the kilim. This technique is used throughout Anatolia.

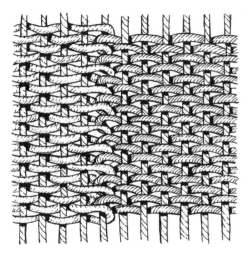

Dovetailing

Dovetailing and single-interlock tapestry In dovetailing the weft threads from adjacent colour areas return around the same warp. Although there is now no slit between the two colour areas, the design does become blurred at the edges, a small ridge is formed at the interlock and the weave cannot be as dense as it is when slitweave is used, because of the doubling up of wefts on a single warp. A link of 1:1 of each colour on the same warp is known as dovetailing; higher ratios give a more jagged outline and are called single-interlock tapestry. These techniques are used in Thrace, Persia and Afghanistan, and the kilims produced are double-sided.

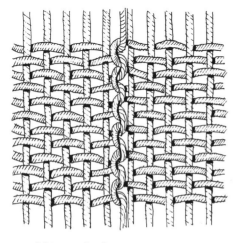

Double-interlock

Double-interlock tapestry This technique is not common in Turkey, but is used extensively in Turkestan and occasionally in Persia, especially among the Bakhtiari tribes. The wefts of adjacent colours link once as they move in one direction and again in the next row in the other direction. This creates a very crisp outline between the colours, and gives a strong, solid weave without slits, but causes a ridge to be formed on the back of the kilim, so that it is not reversible.

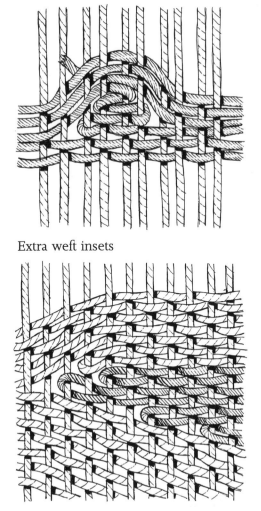

Extra weft insets

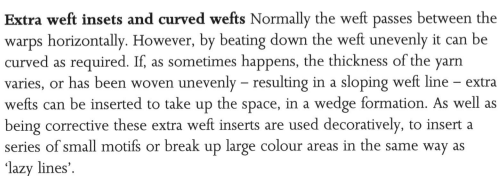

Extra weft insets and curved wefts Normally the weft passes between the warps horizontally. However, by beating down the weft unevenly it can be curved as required. If, as sometimes happens, the thickness of the yarn varies, or has been woven unevenly – resulting in a sloping weft line – extra wefts can be inserted to take up the space, in a wedge formation. As well as being corrective these extra weft inserts are used decoratively, to insert a series of small motifs or break up large colour areas in the same way as 'lazy lines'.

When extra wefts are inserted, the main weft is usually curved around it. This can be skilfully exaggerated by craftsmen so that curvilinear shapes are created, such as waves, or even a perfect circle. Great skill is needed to produce a weave which lies flat despite the variation in tension of the wefts. Curved weft weaving has been extensively used in textiles for many centuries in all corners of the world, and it produces kilims with flowing naturalistic designs, such as those from central and north Persia, rather than the geometric and angular designs that result with slitweave or interlock techniques.

Curved weft

Weft-faced patterning This is a different concept from slitweave, dovetailing or interlocking, where colour changes only occur from one block of colour to the next. With weft-faced patterning, coloured wefts are woven so that they only show on the surface of the kilim when they are needed for part of an intricate pattern that intermingles two or more colours. For the rest of the time, they float along the back of the rug. This technique produces a kilim with distinctive narrow bands of very fine, tightly woven patterns across the width. It is used extensively in Central Asia by Balouch, Qala-i-Nau and Sarmayie weavers. It is occasionally used in Persia and Anatolia in a guard band just next to the fringe.

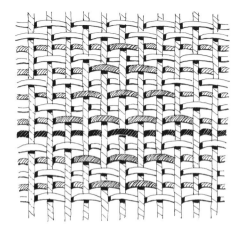

Weft-faced patterning

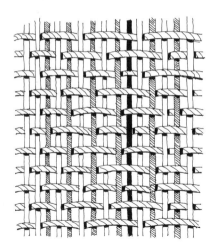

Warp-faced patterning

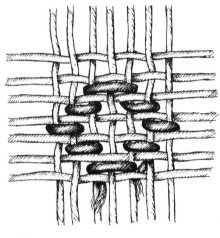

Cicim

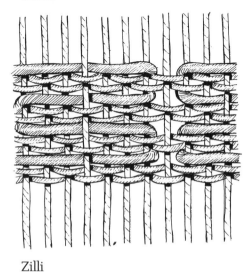

Zilli

Warp-faced patterning A relatively difficult technique not widely used in kilim weaving except in north Afghanistan and parts of Persia. Here the warps form the pattern and colour, and the weft is not visible. When the warp is not being employed on the surface of the weave to produce the pattern it floats along the reverse, as with weft-faced patterning. It is impossible to weave a piece more than about 12 inches wide using the warps in this way because the tension of the weave goes awry. Instead, very long, narrow strips are woven and then cut into equal lengths and sewn together to make a rug. In Central Asia this is called ghujeri. The warp-faced patterning technique is principally used for binding-ropes, tent-bands and long, decorative strips that form a 'cornice' around the top of a room or tent.

Cicim The term cicim is thought to derive from a combination of the Turkish word *cici*, meaning 'small and delightful', and the first person possessive suffix 'im', and it describes a decorative device, often set against a balanced plainweave or weft-faced weave background. Cicim is a technique used mainly in Turkey, although it is occasionally seen in Persian and west Afghan kilims.

It is often mistakenly thought that the extra wefts from which the pattern is formed are embroidered into the piece after the ground weave is finished; in fact, they are interlaced as the whole work progresses. Since the extra yarn is generally thicker than the warp and weft, a raised or couched pattern forms. All cicim designs are in the form of narrow contours of coloured pattern, but these solid line motifs may also be filled in with other kinds of weaving, such as zilli or soumak (see below), or may be woven close together with no ground weave visible in between. Kilims using cicim are often quite lightweight and are traditionally used as curtains, or as furniture and hearth covers.

Zilli Like cicim, zilli is both a Turkish word (meaning 'with small bells or chimes') and a weaving technique found mostly in Anatolia. On the surface of the rug it resembles cording, running parallel with the warps. Extra wefts are wrapped round the warps in a common ratio of 2:1, 3:1 or 5:1. Two or three rows of ground weft are shot between each row of thicker float wefts, so that the surface is completely covered with float over two, three or five warps. Each coloured yarn turns back in its own field, but contours may be created only with the same 'floating three and five' system. One or more warps will be visible where the set has been split between each surface float. In contrast to cicim, zilli is an easy technique for weaving horizontal and vertical lines. Weaving diagonals is a good deal more complicated and can only be done by offsetting the weft floats by a single warp. Zilli is used extensively by Turkish weavers, especially around Konya, Sirrihisar, Canakkale and Mut.

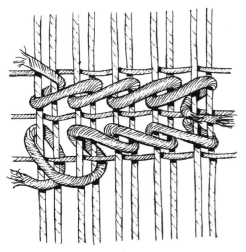

Soumak, counter plain

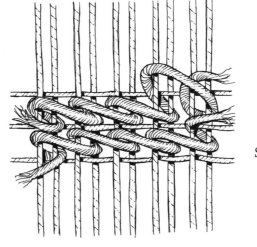

Soumak, ground weft

Soumak The term soumak is said to have derived from the Caucasian town Shemakha, where very fine brocade weft-wrapped kilims have been woven for centuries. The soumak weave is achieved by weft-wrapping rather than the floating or semi-wrapping of extra wefts as in zilli or cicim. Usually it is wrapped with an extra weft in the ground weave, but the most widespread forms of soumak in Anatolia do not have ground weft to support the wrapping structure. The finest soumak kilims come from the Caucasus, and during the last century, from Balouchistan. The technique is not used extensively in Persia or in Turkey except in small areas of weave on bags and juvals. Kilims woven in soumak technique are very hard-wearing and heavy and often display the finest workmanship.

Anatolian prayer kilim (Kagizman)

Chapter Three Recognition and identification

Recognition and identification

Forms, patterns and types

THE RANGE of colours and compositions found in kilims is enormous, from intricate designs in natural, undyed wool to simple, vividly coloured geometric patterns. Kilim owners are often able to trace the origins of their rugs back to a particular tribe, area or town, and many styles can be clearly and easily identified once you know what to look for. The great charm of kilims is that you do not need to be a learned rug expert or academic to be able to spot certain characteristics and pinpoint their origins.

The exact sources of many types are still far from clear, and are debated hotly by collectors, dealers and owners alike. In the Middle East and Central Asia, history is enshrined in the oral tradition of tribal folklore, and few tribes have enjoyed peace and stability for any length of time – a situation which militates against a rigid and academic approach.

This chapter will begin with a look at ways of interpreting the ancient symbols and motifs found on kilims, and with a description of the more unusual forms, such as prayer rugs, bags and runners, that are sometimes available in the West. Finally, there is a comprehensive guide to every major kilim type, starting in Anatolia and moving east towards Afghanistan, following the zig-zag path of the ancient trade routes, describing the colours, patterns and materials used in antique, old and new rugs from all the main areas of production. Kilims typical of each region are described and illustrated in full colour, beginning on p. 70.

Motifs and symbolism

The opening words of the Qur'an are 'There is no God but God' – everything in Islam derives from God and everything represents him, with the result that symbolism in Islamic art is subjective and implicit, and is open to many interpretations. It is certain that many of the symbols that are commonly used in kilims pre-date Islam by many centuries, going back to the very origins of flatweaves in pre-Islamic Central Asia, and to the Animistic and Shamanistic traditions and beliefs of the early pastoral nomads in the southern steppes.

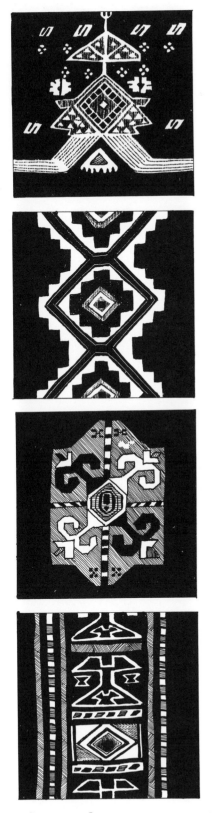

Kilim motifs

The rise of the Islamic faith brought strictures against many of the ancient images used in all forms of art and crafts. The belief that only God can create a living thing was strictly enforced, and the idolatry of early Animistic beliefs was rigorously suppressed. However, representational art was not forbidden by the Qur'an, only idolatry, so the dividing line between forbidden and acceptable images was, as always, indistinct. Weavers avoided the taboo of reproducing the animate, but still incorporated pre-Islamic symbols that had been in use for generations, passed down like folk-tales.

Such symbols have survived the test of time, and formed a language of their own. There is no representation of the Deity in Islam, either in the form of the written word, or through the depiction of people (man being made in God's image). An early Christian tapestry might show God, or the disciples, or tell a story of war and heroism, and contain lifelike images of flowers, trees and animals. The textile would recreate light, shade and a degree of perspective and would attempt to disguise its own form and structure by presenting an illusory pictorial reality.

Not so an Islamic textile. In Islamic art some figurative forms, human and animal, are permitted, but in many cases it is considered disrespectful to walk over them, thus precluding their use in knotted rugs and kilims. For the tribal weavers, however, connections with their natural environment, with their animals and with their family groups are very strong and deeply rooted, and will override religious taboo, so that recognizable objects are depicted in their rugs, but these will never be seen to form part of a complete, pseudo-realistic picture. Art for art's sake is a concept alien to Islam, but kilims are practical as well as decorative, so they are of a high order within the definition of Islamic art.

The motifs and designs on a kilim often hold the key to its age and origins, and can develop out of many different influences and disciplines – for instance, the different weaving techniques often determine the style of the motifs used. Slitweave produces abstract, stepped or crenellated patterns, usually diamond-shaped or triangular; cicim and zilli produce geometric, brocaded 'medallions' in the field of the rug; weft-faced patterning gives a narrow band of geometric and floral patterns across the width of the rug, and soumak is able to produce flowing patterns, representing recognizable images with some accuracy. Kilim weavers have, over the generations, developed ways of combining weaving techniques to achieve more complicated and elaborate designs.

There are two factors other than religion that influence the designs that

45

Scorpion or spider motif

Animal motifs

Jug motif

Elibelinde ('hand on hip') motif

Helicopter motif

a weaver will choose for her kilim. One is the discipline of the weaving techniques themselves, which produce mostly abstract patterns; the other is the natural environment in which the weaver lives, and from which she will adapt motifs to represent lakes, rivers, flowers, petals, trees and leaves, or domestic animals (sheep, goats and camels), wild animals and insects (snakes, scorpions and spiders). She will incorporate images from her own household, such as a kettle, teapot, ewer, comb, beater or lamp, as well as, more recently, objects of Western influence, including cars and bikes and, most recently, even helicopters and automatic rifles.

Knotted carpets and kilims share many symbols and design elements, despite the complete dissimilarity in their weaving techniques. The Anatolian motif 'elibelinde' (meaning 'hand on hip') is seen frequently on both flatweave and pile rugs, as are the 'gol' (lake) and 'gul' (flower). It is difficult to decide whether these motifs first appeared on kilims and were then transferred to knotted carpets, or vice-versa, although quite probably their first origins were in flatweaves. Some motifs, however, certainly originated on knotted carpets and were later used by kilim weavers, such as the flower and leaf patterns that are common to north Persian kilims and knotted rugs alike.

Symbols used in all forms of Asian and Islamic art hold a particular fascination for the West, and there is always a good deal of speculation as to their meaning.

Very often, an original form representing an animate object has evolved through generations of weaving into a stylized pattern. The Western interpretation of this stylized motif is easily misdirected since it calls for a thorough understanding of the concepts of the ancient weavers. Westerners should guard against romanticizing notions of ethnic symbolism and religious significance, which often confuse the theology and images of very different cultures. This is further complicated by the various languages, and

Guls

Tree motif

Comb and tree motif

religious and ethnic origins of the people in Anatolia, Persia and Central Asia. Over the years many of the original interpretations of a motif have changed or been forgotten, different interpretations of the same motif have arisen because of particular local beliefs, and similar motifs are often given different names in different areas.

Another problem is the tendency for Western eyes to see any and all geometric designs in flatweaves as stylizations or corruptions of an original curvilinear and more representational form. Many of the patterns are just geometric forms which have been given descriptive names by which they can be easily identified. Such names have become part of the language of the weavers and later been misinterpreted as signifying an original representational motif. To give an example: the motif used on many Central Asian and Turkoman kilim borders, the 'tree', is a convenient geometric pattern which complies with all the requisites of slitweave – it has short slits and a stepped, crenellated design. It is not a representation of a tree, but it does resemble one, vaguely, and so it is convenient to give it a name by which it can be easily identified and described. More complex, and intriguing, examples of this are the so-called 'lover's quarrel' and 'pair of birds' motifs, or the double-hooked 'ram's horns' and 'camel's neck' symbols.

Lover's quarrel motif

Pair of birds motif

Ram's horns motif

Camel's neck motif

47

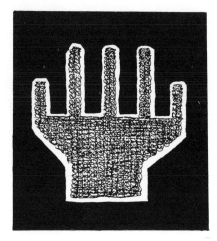

Hand motif

Eye motif

A pattern or design can also be given different names and interpretations in different regions. The narrow guard strip frequently used on many kilims to separate the field from its major borders is colloquially known as a 'ladder'. The same feature, when seen on Turkoman carpets from Central Asia, is known as 'camel's teeth'. The boteh is a very common design element frequently referred to as a hook, curl, peacock or bird's head, and the 'hand motif', sometimes identified as the signature of a particular weaver, is often said to be a representation of the five pillars of Islam, or the prophet Mohammed and his four Caliphs, or the hand of Fatima.

Perhaps the most familiar motif used on kilims and knotted rugs is the 'Tree of Life'. Closer to the true nature of symbolism, this Tree of Life has multiple interpretations and meanings, such as the presence of water in desert lands, or the family tree, with the 'father' trunk and the 'child' branches. Another genuinely symbolic motif is the talismanic evil eye, or 'nazarlik', used to deflect evil and to balance the adverse effects of other motifs on the kilim, such as the spider or scorpion.

On many modern kilims, made in the last thirty years or so, ancient motifs have been misrepresented, or given a new twist, because the weaver has not been aware of the origins of the design she is using. Modern weavers often work from 'cartoons' or pictures of old rugs, recreating them for an enthusiastic Western market. Original motifs will be modified in this process to suit a pre-ordained shape or weaving technique, and so the evolution of the ancient design continues under modern conditions.

Unusual forms

Prayer kilims The devout Muslim must wash his hands, face and feet, find a 'pure' surface and prostrate himself in prayer five times a day. The prayer kilim, with its distinctive mihrab or 'prayer niche' composition, is ideal as a small, transportable and clean surface that may be laid on the ground, with the top of the mihrab pointing to Mecca. It must be said that any clean floor mat, kilim or carpet can be used for prayer, but the mihrab design provides a specific focus and a link with Islamic spiritual traditions. But even the mihrab symbol can be variously interpreted. Its origins can be traced to the arch that is found at the centre of the wall that faces Mecca in all mosques, and prayer kilims are therefore sometimes used as mosque door hangings and decorations.

Prayer kilims are found throughout Anatolia, Kurdistan, Khorasan and west Afghanistan. They form an important part of the weaver's dowry and are often woven for the head of a family or as a gift to the local mosque. Single-arch prayer kilims are of a common size, about 5 feet by 3 feet, but the shapes of the mihrab vary enormously. There are, at one extreme, elaborate architectural forms supported by columns, often with ornate lamp and tree decorations, such as can be seen in central Anatolian examples. These contrast with the simplified and almost unnoticeable mihrabs of the west Afghanistan prayer kilims. Kilims featuring multiple arches, known as 'saf', are rare and exclusive to Anatolia. Their large size, about twelve or fourteen feet long with up to seven niches in horizontal or vertical rows, implies a family use or a decorative function.

Soffrai and rukorsi These are distinctively shaped kilims, largely woven by Kurdish and Balouch tribes. Soffrai, in Persian, means 'small rug'. They take the form of small runners, above five feet in length and about one-and-a-half feet wide, or squares used as eating cloths. Both types are easily indentifiable by their zig-zag motifs, penetrating two sides of a plain, madder red or camel-hair field. The borders are frequently of soumak or knotted work, and these delicate techniques perfectly complement the plain ground. Soffrai runners are woven by the Balouch as 'fill-in' rugs, to lay around the edges of a large room-sized carpet. Rukorsi kilims, about four feet square, are used as covers for charcoal braziers or bread ovens. In the depths of winter, layers of felt topped by a rukorsi kilim make a warm family blanket.

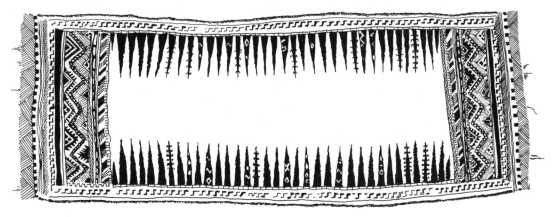

Soffrai

Rukorsi

Bags Tapestry-woven bags are made alongside kilims for practical everyday, but very different uses. Nomadic peoples and settled tribes in villages have little use for furniture, except for low chairs and tin or wooden chests, so flatwoven bags are used for storage and transport. Double bags, known as hurgin or khoorjeen in Persian, and heybe in Turkish, are slung over the shoulder as a small pannier for vegetables and foodstuffs; larger bags, up to three feet square, are set across the backs of camels and donkeys as saddle packs. Bedding and clothing bags include the cradle-like maffrash of Anatolia and the Caucasus, and the pairs of juvals from Khorasan and Afghan Turkestan. Similar to, but smaller than juvals, the Turkoman jaloor bags have long tassels and, like the juvals, are hung on the frame of the yurt for storage. Salt bags, namak donneh, are most distinctive in shape, with a long narrow neck that may be folded over to seal the bag and preserve the valuable contents from moisture.

Jaloor

Characteristics of kilim-producing areas

THRACE

B L A C K   S E A

Sarkoy • Istanbul

• Manastir

• Balikesir

A E G E A N • Bergama

• Ankara

• Sivas

• Bayburt • Kars
• Bardiz
Erzurum

• Aydin

• Obruk
• Konya

• Kayseri

• Malatya

LAKE VAN • Van

T a u r u s   M t s.

Mut •

Reyhanli •

• Aleppo

M E D I T E R R A N E A N

Anatolia

Over this mountainous landmass that is now Asiatic Turkey, East and West have met, traded and clashed for thousands of years. Anatolia is truly the bridge and crossroads between Europe and Asia, and the intermingling of peoples and cultures that has always been a part of its atmosphere continues today. The population of modern Turkey is a mix of Kurds, Armenians, Assyrians, Yoruk and Turkic peoples, Greeks and many others. Of these, the Yoruk and the Kurds have made and continue to make most of the kilims from Anatolia as part of a great tribal and family tradition.

The Kurds The Kurdish peoples are some of the oldest inhabitants of Asia Minor, having lived in the area for over 4000 years; they are of Aryan descent, and are also found in parts of Iran, Syria, Soviet Central Asia and Iraq. Their fractious, mercenary nature and remote, mountainous habitat have ensured their survival through the ages; their conflict with the governments of Turkey, Iraq and Iran continues to this day. The Kurds are famous for the quality and quantity of their kilims, but so many patterns have been attributed to them that no simple

classification is possible. Kurdish homelands straddle the busy east-west caravan routes and the weavers have assimilated and copied patterns from a multitude of sources. The obscure origins of their design and the spread of the Kurdish tribes across the whole of Asia Minor have effectively given puzzled collectors and experts an attributional safety-net: many unusual kilims have, over the years, been labelled as Kurdish for want of any other more final or accurate source.

The Turkic tribes In relatively recent history, during the sixth century, the Turkic tribespeople came to Anatolia out of Central Asia. They are direct ancestors of the dominant tribe of present-day Turkey – the Turks. The first of the Turkic peoples to migrate were the Huns, who settled enormous tracts of Asia from the Yellow River to the Danube. They were followed by successive waves of tribes, pressured out of the east by the Mongols and restrained in the west by the Christians. Most Turkomen remained migratory in habit, and this led to their proud title of Yoruk, meaning 'we who roam'. To this day, despite the fact that there are few truly nomadic or even

51

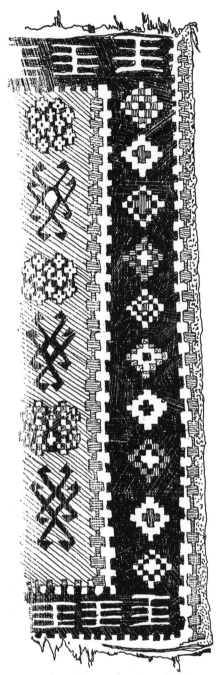

Border of an Anatolian kilim

semi-nomadic peoples in Anatolia, many clans and villages cling to their Yoruk title as an indication of their true Turkic origins.

In Anatolian history it was the Seljuk Turks, arriving in the eleventh century, who established the first of the Turkic empires in Asia Minor. Under the Sultan Tugrul Bey the Byzantines, the reigning power of the time, were defeated on the western shores of Lake Van and the Seljuk empire continued to expand from its capital, Baghdad. Their southward movement into Palestine was the cause of the First Crusade of 1069-99. In the twelfth century the Seljuk Turks moved their capital to Konya in Anatolia, which soon became a centre of Islamic culture and learning. Some of the ancient tribal symbols of the Seljuk can be clearly seen in the kilims produced in the Konya/ Obruk region. However the Turkic and Islamic domination of Asia Minor has since resulted in abstract kilim designs, and in the geometrification of natural forms, such as animals and plants. As ever there is a complex and inadequately charted evolution of designs, mixing a pagan past with the rigid geometric patterns of Islam. Add to this the propensity of the Sultans of the Seljuk and Ottoman empires to move tribes about all over Anatolia, for their own political and military reasons, and you have a melting-pot of design confusion.

The Seljuk empire in Anatolia was shortlived; Konya was taken by the Third Crusade, the twelve sons of one sultan carved the region into provinces and the new force from out of the Asian steppes, the Mongols, were rolling back the eastern frontier. By the beginning of the fourteenth century, the Seljuk empire was fragmented and disunited; meanwhile, displaced from their Central Asian homelands by the advance of the Mongol hordes, another group of Turkic peoples entered Armenia: the Ottomans. They were to rule Anatolia for over 600 years.

The original Ottoman group was led by Suleyman Shah whose son, Ertugrul, was awarded lands after assisting the

Seljuks to victory in a battle with the Mongols. So began the Ottoman dynasty; from the early decades of winning land from the Seljuks and battling with the Mongols, the empire expanded into Europe, conquering Thrace and Bulgaria by 1389. The rejuvenated Mongols under Timurlaine retook most of Asia Minor, with Ankara falling in 1403, but as the Europeans failed to take up the advantage by attacking from the west, this last Mongol rampage was only a setback in the history of the Ottoman empire. By 1566 its lands extended from Hungary in the west to parts of Persia and Iraq in the east, and from the Red Sea to the Crimea. From the death of Suleyman II, the Magnificent, in that year, this huge empire fell into decline. Over the three hundred years that followed, the lands of the Ottoman empire were slowly reduced and this denudation was accelerated to a climax by the First World War. The borders of modern Turkey were established in 1922.

The sophistication and wealth of the Ottoman empire, and especially the tastes of the court élite, had a considerable effect on the designs of kilims. Their legacy is a historic, invaluable collection of written records and some textile fragments that together provide a guide to the more recent history of Anatolian kilims.

The earliest known Anatolian kilims are the floral-patterned Ottoman flatweaves made in the sixteenth century in the Usak area for a specifically urban and courtly marketplace, and the records of the sixteenth and seventeenth-century Ottoman palaces and courts list kilims as decorations, though no indication is given of their provenance. The surviving court kilims are exquisitely made, most probably in a commercial workshop to a commissioned design, and are strongly floral and curvilinear, with patterns of carnations, roses, tulips and hyacinths. For the most part, these Ottoman court kilims are treated as a distinct group, and they are different in many ways from tribal kilims. Courtly styles did, however, begin to filter down to some of the Yoruk and village peoples, influencing their designs, albeit it very slowly; an interesting composite style displaying tribal and courtly elements resulted. To Western eyes, the sophisticated, curvaceous, floral designs seem to integrate well with the geometric animal shapes and abstract patterns of tribal kilims, and this was certainly the case up until the late nineteenth century. Since then, however, the tribal weavers have been virtually bombarded with a variety of different, non-traditional influences. This has created several curious, and to some minds not always successful, mixtures of styles, but striking and unusual Anatolian kilims have often resulted.

Today, Anatolia is leading the kilim-producing nations in both the quality and quantity of the modern production. A thriving and increasingly refined tourist and export market has strongly influenced the manufacture of kilims so that within the last five years, many have begun to be produced on a commercial basis, especially in west and central Anatolia. Patterns and colours are becoming geared to Western tastes and, in many cases, this is no bad thing. Western kilim connoisseurs are insisting on the use of traditional designs and vegetable dyes, and perfect modern imitations of old and antique kilims are being woven. Kilims are also made to order, to a buyer's specific requirements, in terms of colours, size, pattern and quantity.

The village production continues, of course, and this satisfies a family and domestic market although the materials and techniques used have been modified. Cotton warps have largely replaced those of wool and animal hair, and in some villages finished kilims are sun-faded or chemically treated to 'antique' the naturally bright, new colours. These Anatolian village kilims can vary considerably in quality and design and, as ever, it is a rare combination of painstaking technique and fine materials

that will result in a superb specimen. Vertical, fixed looms have replaced portable ground frames, the wool used is machine-spun and yarn, whether cotton or wool, is purchased for use ready-dyed and mordanted.

But Western influences will never take over completely. The roots of tribal traditions are deep within the mind of the weaver. An English textile designer friend travelled to Anatolia recently with a design for a kilim that was totally divorced from traditional uses of colour as dictated by the weaving methods. His major difficulty was in finding a weaver who could understand this totally alien and new composition. Why were certain colours appearing where they were, and why were certain shapes, unrelated to traditional methods, being used? Here was a pattern that departed from the in-built and centuries-old methods. The weavers may be able to absorb small design changes within a basically traditional fomat, but it would be impossible for them to change their whole style of expression – even temporarily. Pattern for them makes no sense unless it is an integral part of the whole woven composition.

Thrace Although strictly out of the geographically defined limits of Anatolia, Thrace, an area that is now European Turkey, is thought to be the originating region for many distinctive kilims. At the height of the Ottoman empire, the Thracian province also comprised much of present-day Bulgaria and northern Greece, and the mix of Central European, Greek and Anatolian cultures can clearly be seen in their kilim production. The typical composition is simple, often the Tree of Life in its many forms surrounded by a floral border with animal and leaf motifs. Those from around the town of Sarkoy are of the finest quality.

Bergama and Balikesir Many distinctive kilims of the nineteenth century can be attributed to this area in western Anatolia, now one of the last strongholds of the

Yoruk peoples. Most of the antique Balikesir kilims are patterned with an interlocking grid of blue on a red ground, with dazzling results; one is never sure which colour forms the pattern and which is the background. More recent Balikesir kilims are varied in design, often decorated with medallions of different sizes on a plain ground, with simple side and end borders or skirts.

Manastir It is unusual to find kilims from Anatolia with any area left undecorated and those from the Manastir region are therefore easy to recognize. The kilims have very strong and simple compositions, usually on a tomato-red or black ground with a plain central field decorated with very few designs. The mihrab, the ceremonial mosque archway, is represented in Manastir kilims by a distinct, floating line rather than by a pattern.

Mut The village of Mut lies south of the Taurus mountains, another region of the semi-nomadic Yoruk pastoralists. The kilims from this area are often found with dark warps of goat hair or brown wool. Brightly coloured medallions are set against a red ground, usually a pair of designs in a mirror image.

Aydin Aydin is a town near the Aegean coast, and a productive source of kilims, often woven in two halves and joined together. As with most western Anatolian kilims the Aydin examples are brightly coloured with small patterns.

Konya The town of Konya lies at the south and centre of a most prolific weaving area, that of west-central Anatolia, once known as Karaman. Few, if any, kilims are made in Konya itself; they come from the surrounding area and take their name from the principal town. Konya kilims are made wholly of wool and are distinguished by the frequent use of slitweave; the kilims are often large, woven in two or three pieces, with a predominantly white or cream background colour into which is woven a strong central series of oval-shaped medallions. Many saf, or multi-mihrab kilims were made in this area.

Obruk Obruk is famous for two types of flatweave: kilims woven using the decorative cicim technique and tapestry-woven kilims used as prayer mats. Large quantities of the latter have been produced, and recent examples are easily identified as the designs differ only slightly from their predecessors.

Kayseri The kilims of this central area of Anatolia are very loosely woven and the older examples have a silky and flat texture. Modern Kayseri kilims are

Medallion kilim from Konya

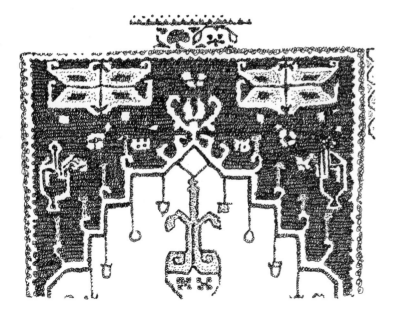

Anatolian prayer kilims

generally red and black, fading to pinks and greys.

Malatya Malatya is in Kurdish country and gives its name to the numerous kilims that are produced in the area by both Kurds and Turkic peoples. Woven in two pieces with warps of white wool, the kilims are usually long, relatively narrow and difficult to make. Commonly, three central medallions are split by the central join, at times most irregularly, and the white sections of the composition are given brilliance by the use of white cotton yarn. Some of the longest Anatolian kilims are found in the Malatya area. Known as band kilims, they can exceed fifteen feet in length and each of the two sections is often, and most unusually for Anatolia, a complete composition in itself. They are sometimes cut and sold as runners. Predominant colours are red and blue with striking white bands.

Sivas/Malatya These kilims are made in the area between Sivas and Malatya in east-central Turkey, by Turkic peoples who are weavers and designers of true genius. The pattern commonly consists of a series of four sections; the colours are gentle and the designs small. The overall effect is of a series of compartments and patterns within patterns that are a delight to the eye.

Sivas Woven by Kurds, most Sivas kilims, and indeed most of the kilims made anywhere east of here, are prayer mats in muted colours with a strong single and central mihrab motif. All are made in one piece and the mihrab is bordered by three narrow bands full of gul designs.

Bayburt and Erzurum These prayer rugs are woven in predominantly yellow or ochre colours with tiered central mihrabs surrounded by stylized floral designs, especially carnations. Many of the kilims have their year of weaving woven into the design. Just east of this area is the village of Bardiz, where most of the Karabagh or modern Bessarabian kilims are made. The Kurdish weavers are excellent copyists and have been producing these large floral-patterned kilims since the 1920s, using European tapestry designs such as those from Aubusson and Savonnerie in France. Curiously, these were themselves derived from the original Ottoman floral kilims of the seventeenth century – a full circle of design ideas.

Van This remote and mountainous district of eastern Anatolia has maintained many clans of semi-nomadic Kurds, largely undisturbed for thousands of years. Most invaders wisely passed by the area and it is only now, after twenty years of increasing tourist penetration and strong central government control, that the original Kurdish lifestyle is disintegrating. Until recently, kilims were made in large numbers entirely for family and local use. The kilims are, unusually, square and are generally in two pieces; many examples bear a resemblance to the kilims of north-west Persia and the Caucasus, made by other Kurdish groups. Kilims from Van are well made, with good quality wool, and will last for many years.

Kars The kilims from this area close by the Russian border are typical of most Kurdish work – either long narrow strips or small prayer rugs. Thick, dark woollen warps give a ribbed effect, and in general, colours are browns, pinks and oranges. Many patterns show a strong Caucasian influence.

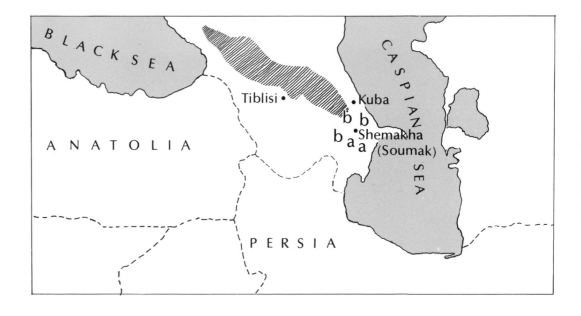

The Caucasus. Shirvan kilim-producing areas are indicated by **a**, Kuba by **b**

The Caucasus

The Caucasus region is now defined as the Soviet Socialist Republics of Azerbaijan, Armenia and Georgia. This is an area sandwiched between the Greater Caucasian range of mountains to the north and the lands of the Kurds to the south. The Kurds are now divided between Turkey, Iran, Iraq and Syria, and they are campaigning for their own independent homeland, Kurdistan.

If Anatolia was a highway and crossroads between cultures, the Caucasus was a motorway and through route. Since ancient times the true Caucasians have endured battles between great empires on their lands, and the settlement of many ethnic minorities in the obscurity of their mountains. The Greeks, Persians, Arabs, Turks and Tartars came and went, leaving a trail of colourful and confusing cultural influences. Until the early nineteenth century, the region had known very little peace for thousands of years. After two

Caucasian scorpion or spider motif

hundred years of conflict, the dispute between the Ottomans and the Persians over possession of the Caucasus was settled by the expansion of the Russian empire. This southward movement drove a wedge between Turkish and Persian interests and began what can now be seen as the Golden Age of carpet and kilim production in the Caucasus. Most if not all kilims date from this peaceful era that began in the early nineteenth century and ended in the aftermath of the Russian Revolution.

Inspired by their newfound political stability and the opening up of new markets by the Russian railroads and sea routes, the tribes of the Caucasus in the nineteenth century created some of the finest slitweave kilims in existence today. These kilims were woven by indigenous Caucasian tribes such as the Avars, Samurs and Georgians, and by the Kurds, Persians, Armenians, Turks and Arabs now permanently settled in the region. Unusually, the kilims were made by both men and women; those from the permanent workshop looms by men, and those from the semi-nomadic tribes by women. In contrast to other kilim-producing areas, there seems to be no clear distinction between the quality and originality of commercial and family weavings. This may be due to the fact that both kinds of kilim production in the area stopped almost completely just as Western influences were beginning to filter through; thus the bulk of Caucasian kilims that we see today were made at a time when commercial pressures and motives were largely unheard of, and traditional tribal designs were invariably still used.

In a region where over ninety different languages are spoken by some three hundred and fifty tribes, it is difficult to pinpoint the origins of many of the flatweaves of the nineteenth century with any degree of accuracy. Kilims are grouped according to design and structure, and the Caucasus as a whole has traditionally been divided by rug connoisseurs into two main regions: Kuba and Shirvan. These titles have become entrenched in rug literature, but there is little hard evidence to support their use. Indeed, many kilims show also the varied influences, cultural and geographical, of the Kurdish, Anatolian and Persian peoples. Out of this confusion certain features are common to all Caucasian kilims: the basic structure of the kilim is all wool and the white designs are often highlighted with undyed cotton. The fabric is pure slitweave of the highest quality, being even, tight and of uniform thickness. Caucasian kilims are woven in one piece and their compositions are based on repeated patterns of geometric motifs, usually saw-toothed medallions arranged in horizontal rows or in a diagonally offset series. The pattern repeat is endlessly inventive, producing a design of great impact – a perfect combination of precision weaving, fine yarn and strong, contrasting dyes.

Kuba Kuba kilims are decorated with large and abstract geometric medallions or cartouches. The composition is usually completed by a border of repeated designs. Few areas remain undecorated in the central field of the kilim; indeed, this frenetic and colourful style is a hallmark of all Caucasian flatweaves.

Shirvan The kilims identified with this region are commonly perceived as the archetypal Caucasian production. Large numbers of high-quality kilims, and bags separated into small kilims, are available. Their colour palette is similar to that of the Kuba, although slightly softer, and the materials used are identical, as is the standard of craftsmanship. Unlike the Kuba, the Shirvan kilims have no borders and display a more abstract treatment of the bold, geometric medallions.

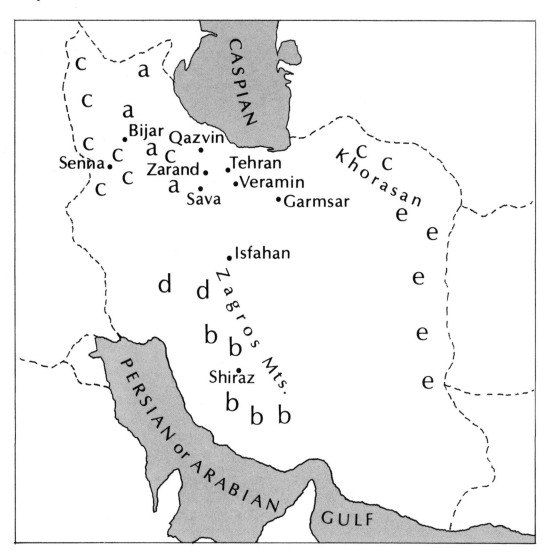

Persia. Kilim-producing tribal areas are indicated as follows: **a** Shahsavan; **b** Qashqai; **c** Kurds; **d** Bakhtiari; **e** Balouch

Persia

If oriental carpets of the seventeenth and eighteenth centuries were invariably described as 'Turkish', then 'Persian' surely stands today as a much abused term, an erroneous synonym for all types of carpets and rugs. But there is, in fact, no real problem in identifying authentic Persian kilims, since their varied tribal ancestry has resulted in sharp colours and strong, abstract patterns, quite different from the fine silk carpets produced in urban workshops, packed with floral and other figurative designs, and available everywhere in the West.

The origins of the Persian tribes can be traced back to the greatest empires of Asia. Persia has been ruled by Achaemenidae, the Greeks, the Sassanian kings, the Arabs, the Mongols and the Turkomen, finally returning to local control with the Safavid dynasties. All have left their mark by way of their tribal enclaves scattered about modern-day Iran. The distribution, over the centuries, of these immigrants from areas such as Central Asia and the Caucasus was thrown into disarray by the Persian monarchs of the seventeenth and eighteenth centuries. Whole tribes were forcibly uprooted from one end of Persia and settled in some remote border district for political and military reasons. The confusion caused by the cultural mixtures and the free movement of tribes across frontiers until relatively recently means that the exact origins of some Persian kilims remain a matter of calculated guesswork.

Most of the finest Persian kilims that can be found today were woven in the nineteenth and early twentieth centuries by Kurdish and Turkic tribes before the repressive regime of Rezah Shah. Kilims were woven for traditional family and domestic purposes within the villages and encampments of the area's many tribes; the highest quality floral patterned kilims were produced in workshops in Senna, the capital of Kurdistan.

The policies of the Pahlavi regime, established in 1925, were directly aimed at reducing the political powers of the tribes of Persia, tribes that were fast dwindling to a minority amongst the Persians of the towns and cities. Tribal leaders were imprisoned, firearms confiscated and nomadic groups forcibly settled on marginal lands that could not support them, or their flocks. For fifteen years after the overthrow of Reza Shah in 1941, the tribespeople enjoyed a return to self-government and traditional lifestyles. After 1956 and to this day the governments of Iran have continued with a tribal settlement and emasculation programme that has attempted to create a

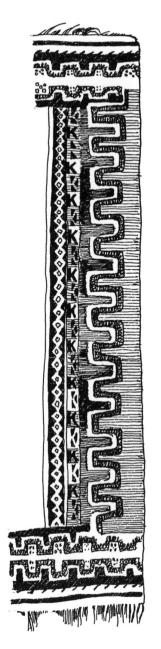

Border of a Persian kilim

homogeneous Iranian society. These actions and the social changes that have occurred because of Westernization of the country have all but destroyed the forces behind the traditional production of kilims, although they continue to be produced in Persia today on a much smaller scale.

Before the Islamic revolution, and as with Anatolian production, there was a strong Western commercial and scholarly pressure to re-introduce vegetable dyes and traditional patterns. Much of this work was concentrated on the weaving of the Qashqai of southern Persia.

Senna Senna, now known as Sandanaj, is the capital of the district called Kurdistan and gives its name to a group of finely woven kilims of the eighteenth, nineteenth and early twentieth centuries. The fine floral patterns were inspired by the embroideries and brocades of the Safavid period and most were workshop produced for a sophisticated urban demand.

Senna kilims are small in size and finely woven in slitweave and eccentric weft technique, with cotton warps and woollen wefts; motifs are frequently enhanced with metal or silk threads. The designs often consist of small clusters of flowers, boteh, running vines, bees and a central diamond cluster of small flowers known as a Herati pattern. Persia is not known for its prayer kilims, the sole exception being those made in Senna, with their distinctive bulbous mihrab. The central field of Senna kilims is flanked by a series of major and minor borders of leaf, stem and other floral motifs. The colours are predominantly blue, red and white.

Bijar These kilims are woven in the villages and nomadic camps of Kurdistan and are often naïve copies of Senna work. The weave is of coarse cotton and wool, the colours are bright, and small animal and human figures are often depicted in the field, with charming results.

Shahsavan The Shahsavan are a confederation of the most important of the Turkic tribes that are found on the north-west Persian border with the Caucasus. Some of the tribal groups are semi-nomadic, moving from the plains of Mughan to the summer pastures in the mountains west of Ardabil. Shahsavan means 'lovers of the Shah', indicating their mercenary attachment to the Safavid rulers, and these Turkic tribes are descended from the Seljuk Turks of Central Asia. Members of this confederation include those Caucasian Turks who fled south from the Russians in the late nineteenth century.

The Shahsavan are best known for their ceremonial horse blankets, woven in soumak technique and decorated with horses, deer and birds. Kilims from this area are similar in design and scale to the southern Caucasian production, differing only in the raw materials used, and in certain design details. Shahsavan kilims are woven with dark, dry and coarse wool, a contrast to the fabled soft, fine and ivory-coloured woollen yarn of the Caucasus. Persian influences are evident in the random scattering of stylized birds, flowers and human figures in the field of the kilim.

Zarand Kilims woven between the villages of Sava, Zarand and Qazvin in central Persia are collectively known as the Zarand production. They are often the work of elements of the Turkic Shahsavan who have settled in the area in large numbers.

Zarand kilims are all long, narrow and durable, woven with cotton warps and a heavy woollen weft. Small slitweave and eccentric weft work are the techniques most commonly used. Patterns are stylized and floral, with running vine and trefoil on the inner and outer borders; colours are muted blues, creams and browns. More often than not the floral motifs group to form a diamond grid pattern, or two or three medallions.

Border of a Kurdish kilim

Veramin and Garmsar Kilims woven in this region, some 35 miles south-east of Tehran, have diverse tribal origins, for the towns of Veramin and Garmsar straddle the east-west trading and migration routes of Central Persia. Arabs, Kurds, Shahsavan, Lurs, Qashqai and many other tribes have mingled here, and have settled and established an important kilim-weaving district.

Veramin and Garmsar kilims are heavy, tightly woven and large in size, with cotton warps or warps and wefts of the local dark and relatively coarse wool. Selvedges are distinctive, forming ridges of dark, cabled warps to the sides of the kilims; weaving techniques include delicate slitweave, lines of weft-faced patterning with 'S' and rosette designs, and weft wrapping to highlight the designs. Compositions include horizontal or diagonally offset bands of motifs or a field of interlocking designs that converge to dazzling effect. Garmsar and Veramin kilims have a colour palette of brilliant reds and blues, and unusual greens and yellows on a dark ground.

Qashqai The nomadic Qashqai of the Fars district of south-west Persia are well known for their traditionally woven kilims. The tribe's origins can be traced back to the sixteenth century, when its people formed part of the Turkic hordes who invaded from the north. As a result, some Qashqai kilim patterns can be directly related to those of the Caucasus.

Once famed for their long annual migration from their winter quarters by the Persian gulf to their summer pastures in the Zagros mountains, the Qashqai have suffered heavily under the repressive policies of the Persian governments since 1925. In consequence, most of the best rugs were woven before the Pahlavi regime, and these older Qashqai kilims are particularly exciting and satisfying to live with.

Woven during migrations, or at resting-places, Qashqai kilims often display striking variations and shifts in pattern and colour. Only a small amount of dyed yarn can be carried by the nomads at any one time, so successive batches of wool for the same kilim have to be dyed en route, hence the colour variations. The ground looms upon which they are woven are often packed up and moved while weaving is in progress, so that the patterns are interestingly varied.

Bakhtiari The Bakhtiari tribes were, until recently, a nomadic group. They migrated from the plains of west-central Persia into and over the Zagros mountains. Their origins are obscure and ancient, their language is Persian and only the inaccessibility of their homelands has ensured the survival of their cultural traditions. Bakhtiari kilims are, therefore, original in design, retaining their tribal identity and purity.

Weaving techniques are unusual. Double interlock is used, with cotton warps and woollen wefts, resulting in one-sided, stiff and strong kilims. The rugs are long and narrow, with clear colours and bright contrasts of yellows, blues, reds and oranges. Designs most commonly consist of a grid pattern of boxes in the field, or a pattern of boteh or lozenge shapes, surrounded by several concentric borders. The ends of the kilims are finished in bands of weft-faced patterning. Horse covers are woven in soumak technique with striking compositions of animal motifs and bands of colour.

Khorasan This region in the north-east of Persia, bordering Afghanistan and Soviet Central Asia, is home to the indigenous Balouch and Turkoman tribes as well as groups of Kurds. These were displaced from their homelands in the Caucasus and Kurdistan by the Ottoman Turks in the sixteenth century and eventually forced to settle in Khorasan to defend Persia against the raiding Uzbeks from Central Asia.

The Kurds weave large brocade kilims with stripes and lattice patterns in dark blues and reds, as well as heavily brocaded and robust bags. It is often difficult to distinguish these Kurdish weaves from the work of related tribes further west.

Many of the Turkomen of Khorasan are exiles from Soviet Central Asia, such as the Tekke and Yomut tribes who fled from Imperial Russia in the nineteenth century, and from the Soviets in the twentieth. Their kilims are distinguished by their deep red ground onto which are brocaded the characteristic Turkoman guls. Flatweaving is confined to large dowry brocades, jaloors and pairs of juvals.

There are also groups of Balouch peoples living in Khorasan, thought to be of ancient Persian stock from the central Kirman region, displaced east and north-east by the Turkic invasions of the eleventh and twelfth centuries. The Balouch who inhabit this borderland between Iran and Afghanistan are known as the Rukhshanis, and they produce many kilims commonly identified as Balouch. By contrast, few kilims are made by the eastern Balouch tribes, the Brahuis of the deserts of Pakistan Balouchistan.

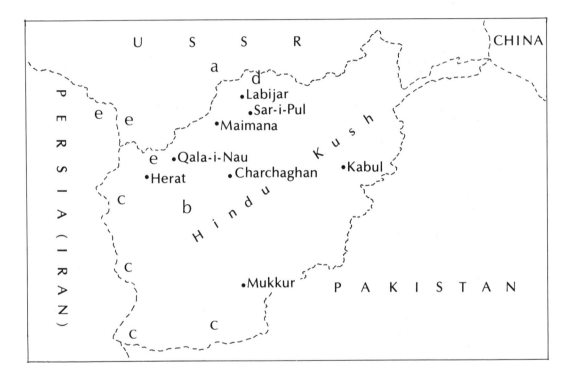

Afghanistan. Kilim-producing tribal areas are indicated as follows: **a** Kazakh; **b** Taimani; **c** Balouch; **d** Tartar; **e** Turkoman

Afghanistan

This land-locked and much fought over country has attracted travellers and conquerors alike; the strong contrasts in the climate and the natural colours of the desert and mountain landscape have been an inspiring source for some of the most unusual Asian kilims. The geographical position of this mountainous landmass, with deep, easily defended ravines and passes, has led empire builders to invade the country from the earliest times. After the

conquest of Persia, Alexander formed a successful self-governing colony of ancient Greece and established the crossroads of trade routes from Cathay and India to Europe. The country later formed part of the Parthian and Sassanian empires, and has at various times been partly subject to both Persia and the Moguls. It has also been divided amongst smaller, native dynasties, the most notable being the Ghazni, in the twelfth century. The interaction, development

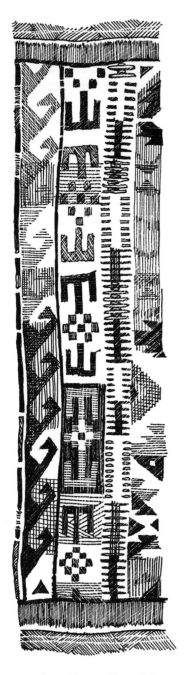

Border of an Afghan kilim

and influence of separate tribal groups, remnants of invading parties and nomadic people continued under centuries of political intrigue. An independent kingdom rose in Kandahar in 1708 and over the next century it expanded to the Persian border in the west and annexed part of the Punjab in the east. However, this kingdom was not without civil unrest and tribal in-fighting, out of which eventually emerged Dost Mohammed in 1823 as the self-styled Amir. Expansionist political pressures from Persia and Russia forced the Amir to request the help of Britain, resulting in the first Afghan War of 1838, and finally independence in 1919. As a result, a political and military scheme of boundaries was imposed onto ancient tribal areas, the repercussions of which are still being felt today.

The kilims of Afghanistan reflect the country; they are tough and hard-wearing. Very little has been written about them, which is surprising since, of all Asian kilims, they are the closest to the very origins of flatweaving and the least affected by outside influences. Patterns are simple and bold, arising naturally from the weaving process. Chemical dyes have been used recently, and a particularly vivid orange was popular among weavers in the 1970s. Overly bright or artificial colours should be treated with caution by the collector, though it is still possible to find nomadic weavings that make use of good vegetable dyes. Kilims from Afghanistan can be pinpointed to particular areas of origin, but there are some problems. This is one of the crossroads of the world, with a mêlée of people from different tribes. There are the Aimaq or Chahar Aimaq, the Turkomen and the Hazara, plus many tribal subdivisions, and it is not always easy to identify places and names of tribal areas with any degree of certainty. Because a large proportion of the people in Afghanistan are nomadic, names often become duplicated or confused, and the various languages – Pashtun, Farsi or a local dialect –

compound the difficulty. Generally, the main tribal name or the name of the principal market town or village in an area can be used for identification.

Balouch Much of Balouchistan is sparsely populated and arid, with fiercely contrasting summer and winter weather. It is an extensive and loosely defined tribal area that extends from Herat and Mashed in the north, to the Dasht-i-Margo – 'desert of death' – in the south, and to Quetta and the edge of the Sind desert in the east. The warps of Balouch kilims are all wool, with the exception of those from the Persian Balouch who sometimes use cotton. Colours are very dark, sombre browns, deep purples and reds, with delicate, contrasting white patterns in cotton, woven into the weft in bands across the rug. The quality of pattern is very subtle, contained in the texture of the weave as well as in the colour, and it responds beautifully to careful lighting. There are two main groups of Balouch people, the Rukhshanis, who originated from the south of the Caspian Sea, and the Brahuis, who settled in the western deserts of Afghanistan after being driven from north India by the Aryan invasion in the fifteenth century. The Balouch are mainly semi-nomadic, with several true nomadic sub-clans. The women do all the weaving, using wool from the Balouch and Ghilzai flocks in the south, and from the Karaqul breeds near Herat in the north. The weaving is carried out on ground looms, and long, narrow strips are sewn together to make a wider rug. Weft-faced patterns and soumak technique are invariably used. As well as kilims, the Balouch are noted for their saddle and storage bags, often embellished with white glass beads from Herat, mother-of-pearl buttons and cowry shells. They are among the finest weavers in the world, and their heavy, tightly woven kilims are extremely hard-weaving.

Qala-i-Nau This is a small town north-east of Herat where Sunni Muslims of the Chahar Aimaq tribe live. Their weavings are in many ways similar to Balouch kilims, but are very finely and ornately patterned. They always use weft-faced patterning, so that the rugs are characterized by narrow bands of colour and pattern. They are invariably woven from Karaqul wool on narrow ground looms. A distinguishing feature is a 'barber-pole' design over-embroidered on the selvedge edges and across wide plainweave ends.

Taimani In the deep valleys between the Farah and Hari Rud rivers, in central west Afghanistan, are the Taimani. A semi-nomadic people originating from the Aimaq tribe, they weave mainly soumak-type rugs, though more recently they have produced pieces with a combination of soumak and knotted pile. Many of the modern rugs have patterns drawn from traditional designs, such as boteh, but representational images of helicopters, pistols and Kalashnikov rifles also figure, in a new folk art reflecting the turmoil of the war. The wool comes from Ghilzai sheep owned by Pashtun shepherds. Colours are varied, but dark red and purple are often used.

Sarmayie These kilims are woven by the pastoralist Chahar Aimaq people (Aimaq is a Mongolian word, meaning nomad). They are found near Charchaghan, the capital of Ghor province in central-west Afghanistan. Soft browns and yellows are woven into bands composed of diamond-shaped patterns. The rugs are made in one piece and are unusually wide, considering they are woven on ground looms by itinerant weavers.

Mukkur This small town in the south of Afghanistan, near Kandahar, is the bazaar of the Pashtun-speaking nomadic tinkers of Afghanistan, the Koochi. These are one of Central Asia's last nomadic tribes, and they embellish their textiles, clothes, utensils and animal trappings with bright

Rifle motif

embroidery, beads, mirrors and shells. Their kilims are long, narrow and robustly woven in slitweave with a strong geometric pattern. The wool yarn is thickly spun, so the rugs are heavy but flexible. Very often one can find blue glass beads woven into the large end tassels, or small mirrors, metal discs and metallic wire embroidered into the weave.

Turkoman The Turkomen are renowned as tough horsemen, traders and traditional weavers from the Kara Kum – the Great Desert – on the southern steppes of Russia, Afghanistan and Iran. Of the fifty or so tribes and sub-tribes that make up the Turkoman people, only four are recognized as kilim weavers: the Salor, Tekke, Yomut and Ezari.

Most Turkomen in Afghanistan arrived there in the early 1920s as refugees from Communism and suppression in southern Russia, between the Aral Sea and Persia. Turkomen are famed the world over as weavers of fine knotted pile carpets, and the colours and patterns of their kilims closely resemble these. Deep madder red and reddish-brown are the predominant colours, with brocaded guls, distinctive to each tribe, woven in dark brown or black wool. The kilims are unusually large, about twelve or fourteen feet long.

Labijar The Labijar are a group of villages on the edge of a large irrigation complex in central Afghan-Turkestan. Their kilims, similar in weight and density to those from Maimana, use slitweave and dovetailing techniques, and are easily recognized by a square grid of panels of rich madder or indigo colour with a striking gold double-headed arrow motif in the centre. They are usually very large and hard–wearing. Recently, the 'Christmas tree' motif, also traditional to Labijar, has been copied by the Uzbeks of Sar-i-Pul.

Maimana kilim

Sar-i-Pul In the very centre of Afghanistan, on the northern slopes of the Hindu Kush, Sar-i-Pul is set in a fertile, lush area inhabited by Hazara people, who are supposedly direct descendants from the armies of Ghengis Khan, left to maintain peace in this part of his empire. They are devout Shi'ah Muslims. The Hazaras are poor – even relative to other parts of Afghanistan – and being mainly arable farmers, have few flocks of their local breed of sheep, the Hazarangi. Their kilims are generally long and narrow, and are unusual in that they have large areas of white or ivory flatweave, with small dashes of colour and contrasting horizontal bands of colourful diamonds and zig-zags. In the nearby areas of Mazar and Behsud, very hard-wearing kilims are woven. These often have very little patterning, usually showing wide bands of undyed coloured wool (white, black or brown), with occasional bands of chemical purple- or red-dyed wool. The end borders are usually of natural brown wool.

Maimana The provincial capital of Maimana in north–west Afghanistan is a collecting point and bazaar for kilims from a large surrounding area of Turkestan and Afghan-Turkestan. Originally Maimana kilims were woven by Uzbeks, but now they have been copied by the Aimaqs. They are often quite large, up to one hundred square feet, and are woven indoors on vertical looms, or in a yurt tent specially built to contain the loom. Slitweave or dovetailing are invariably used and the kilims are easily recognizable by their simple geometric pattern of diamonds and triangles in the field (the central section of the composition), together with wide borders incorporating many traditional designs, such as the tree, scorpion and comb. The colours are also strong: reds, oranges, blues, rusty browns and yellows are predominantly used.

Tartari The Uzbek Tartars create distinctive kilims in double interlock weave, using only the finest spun wool. The field of the rug invariably features a repetitive eight-legged spider motif, in yellows, greens and blue. The border consists of a distinctive zig-zag, often varying in size and colour as the weaver works on the rug over a period of weeks or months.

Uzbek Uzbekistan is another of the ancient districts of Soviet Central Asia, which was populated by Turkic nomads and invaded by empire builders and marauders, so that the present-day inhabitants display many different origins and tribal groupings. The Uzbeks who migrated to Afghanistan in the early twentieth century now copy many traditional designs, but the true Uzbek kilim, called a ghujeri, is woven in brightly coloured strips of warp-faced patterning, cut into lengths and sewn together.

Kazakh Kazakhistan is located upon a remote, arid steppe – the Kilil Kum desert – in east Soviet Central Asia. The semi-nomadic people are Turkic speaking, of Mongol descent, sometimes known as Lakai. They live a tough, pastoralist life in traditional yurts (circular tents), as they have done since settling in this region in the thirteenth and fourteenth centuries. The Kazakh women are primarily felt makers – simple but boldly decorated floor mats and coverings for the yurt – but in recent years they have started to weave heavy soumak kilims. Predominantly red and orange in colour, the kilims are easily identified by their coarsely-spun yarn, thick brown sheep's wool fringes and distinctive, repetitive gul designs, outlined in black.

Herds of sheep and goats are staple to every nomad and semi-nomad in the Middle East and Central Asia. Sources for natural dyestuffs are scarce in this barren, mountainous landscape, and kilims are often woven in the natural brown, red, cream and black colours of the undyed fleeces.

A Kirghiz woman from north Afghanistan weaving a tent band or narrow strip that may be cut and joined to others to make a ghujeri. She is working with the traditional ground loom, used for centuries without change for the majority of nomadic weavings. The warp threads are stretched between beams pegged to the ground. A tripod of roughly carved poplar wood poles supports the heddle and the weaver sits on her completed work to provide the correct tension to the threads being worked.

Opposite. Weaving in this north Syrian village has taken on the appearance of a cottage industry, employing the whole family. The large, relatively sophisticated horizontal loom is permanently installed under cover and skeins of chemically dyed wool are being prepared for weaving.

Kilims are rolled or folded and packed onto the backs of camels or donkeys when a nomadic or semi-nomadic tribe is on the move. The scene (right), near Herat in Afghanistan, is typical. Woven bands of varying widths are used to lash packs and utensils onto the domestic animals. They are also used to wrap the barrel frame of the traditional yurt tent (below). Large kilims are frequently woven as gifts and laid over the floors of mosques as an act of faith, as in this mosque in the Turkish town of Konya (opposite).

Anatolia and the Caucasus

Thrace The 'Tree of Life' composition is most common in kilims from this region of Turkey. A floral border with animal and leaf motifs is typical, and red and blue colours predominate.
Size: 7′6″ × 4′6″.

Bergama and Balikesir Antique and old kilims from western Anatolia are recognized by the interlocking patterned grid of blue on a red ground. Modern Balikesir rugs are varied in design, often featuring a plain ground decorated with medallions of varying sizes. Size: 10′0″ × 4′0″.

Manastir Very simple compositions with little patterning make Manastir kilims easy to distinguish from the usual highly patterned Anatolian varieties. The colour of the ground is usually tomato-red or black. Size: 5′3″ × 3′3″.

Aydin Like most western Anatolian kilims, those from *Aydin* (right) have small-scale busy patterns in bright colours. They are often woven in two halves and joined together. Size: 10′0″ × 5′3″.

Mut The kilims of Mut (above) are often found with dark warps of goat hair or sheep's wool. Mirror images of brightly coloured medallions, with a contrasting crenellated band of dark wool, are set against a red ground. Size: 6′6″ × 3′6″.

Konya Kilims attributed to the Konya area are woven in large quantities in the surrounding villages. Made entirely of wool, using slitweave technique, these large kilims are made up from two or even three pieces sewn together, with a white or cream ground and a series of medallions down the centre (above). Konya is also a centre for modern workshop productions of good quality, such as the one pictured here (left). Sizes: 14′0″ × 6′0″ (above), 5′0″ × 3′0″ (left).

71

Obruk Kilims produced in Obruk (above) have large, repetitive designs. Cruciform and small medallion patterns make up two or three borders. The mihrab on prayer kilims is well proportioned and pointed. Rugs are woven in bright, light colours – blues, greens and reds. Obruk also produces kilims woven using the decorative cicim technique (right). Sizes: 6′4″ × 3′10″ (above), 8′9″ × 5′6″ (right).

Kayseri Loosely woven in slitweave, with contour bands reinforcing the structure, these kilims from central *Anatolia* (above) are usually red and black in colour, fading to softer pinky-browns and greys with age, as here. Size: 7′6″ × 4′6″.

Malatya These kilims are woven by the Kurds and Turks of the Kurdish district in two matched halves. The intricately made and patterned rugs here (top right) have three central medallions with contrasting white cotton areas. Band kilims from Malatya (right) are woven in separate halves, each one complete in itself. These are then joined, and the resulting rugs are some of the longest to be found anywhere. They are dark red and blue in colour, with striking bands of white patterning. Sizes: 11′0″ × 5′0″ (top right), 11′6″ × 4′9″ (right).

Sivas/Malatya These very finely woven kilims are easily recognized by their series of compartmentalized patterns within patterns (above). Woven in slitweave technique, loosely outlined with weft wrapping, they are rich and varied in colour and design. Size: 12′0″ × 4′6″.

73

Sivas *Invariably prayer rugs, these kilims (above) are woven in soft, muted colours with a strong central mihrab design, and borders full of highly decorative gul, or flower, designs.*
Size: 6'9". × 3'3".

Karabagh *To the east of Erzurum, Karabagh and modern Bessarabian kilims are made (top right). Designs are floral, colours are strident. This rug clearly displays the use of 'lazy lines' in the red field of the mihrab. Size: 5'9" × 4'0".*

Erzurum *Prayer kilims with distinctive floral designs of life-like carnations and leaves (right). Very often, their date of composition is woven into the design. They are yellow and ochre in colouring. Size: 6'6" × 5'0".*

Modern facsimile kilim *A modern eastern Anatolian prayer kilim (above) copying antique west Anatolian and Thracian designs. This woollen kilim is beautifully made and coloured with vegetable dyes. Size: 6'6" × 4'3".*

Kuba Large abstract diamond-shaped medallions, the hallmark of Caucasian kilims, are always found in Kuba kilims (left). They are decorated with strong, colourful slitweave patterns.
Size: 12′0″ × 5′0″.

Kars Typical of most Kurdish work, these kilims are usually prayer rugs, or composed of long strips sewn together (above left). They have dark woollen warps and strong, dark patterns.
Size: 11′0″ × 5′0″.

Van Woven in two strips, kilims from around Lake Van are well made from good, hard-wearing wool (left). They resemble kilims woven by other Kurdish groups in the Caucasus and north-west Persia, being finely patterned with dark ground colour. Size: 6′3″ × 5′2″.

Shirvan Identified by their bold diamond-shaped medallions in bands across the kilim, most Shirvan rugs have no border, as here (above). Wool, techniques and sizes are identical to those from Kuba, though the colours are softer.
Size: 7′0″ × 4′0″.

75

Persia

Senna Senna kilims are usually small in size and very finely woven, with small clusters of flowers, boteh and bees covering the field. Narrow borders are patterned with a running vine motif. Sometimes, the field may display a central diamond-shaped cluster of small flowers, or herati. Pictured are a village-produced kilim (top right) and a workshop kilim (right) featuring floral boteh in the central field. Sizes: 6'0" × 3'6" (top right), 7'1" × 4'8" (right).

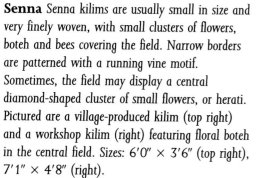

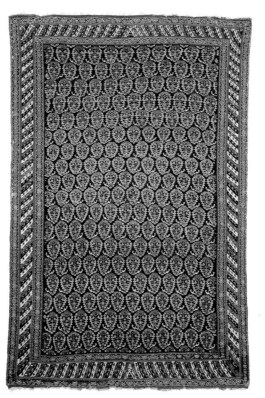

Bijar In this Kurdish area of north-west Persia, the kilims are usually woven with coarse wool wefts and cotton warps. The colours are bright, with strong patterns, which are sometimes decorated, as here (above), with representations of human figures and animals. The shape is usually long and narrow, and naïve copies of Senna kilims are often woven in this area. Size: 10'9" × 3'9".

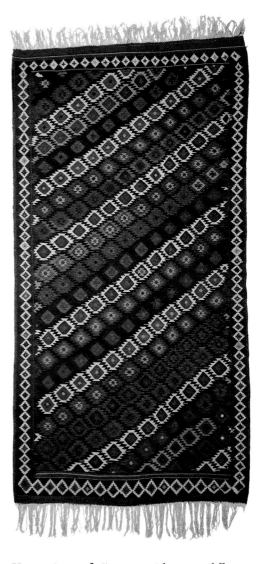

Shahsavan saddle cover *The Shahsavan are best known for their ceremonial horse blankets woven in soumak technique. They are decorated with representations of horses, deer and birds. Kilims from this area are woven in dry, coarse wool, in dark colours, with similar representations of animals and birds scattered in the field. Size: 4'9" × 4'9".*

Zarand *Long, narrow and durable, Zarand kilims are woven in tight slitweave with eccentric weft work, incorporating varied and stylized flowers, running vines and trefoil patterns formed around two or three diamond-shaped medallions (right). Colours are soft, muted blues, creams and browns. Size: 11'6" × 3'3".*

Veramin and Garmsar *The many different people settled in this prolific kilim-producing area weave an astonishing variety of kilims. They are usually heavy and tightly woven with diamond motifs (above) or interlocking triangular designs that are dazzling to look at. Size: 11'0" × 5'0".*

Qashqai For centuries the Qashqai have been prolific weavers of distinctive kilims (facing page, above and right). Motifs and patterns often resemble those of the Caucasus, although in brighter colours, and there are also more unusual designs, pictured here, with large, diamond-shaped medallions and 'chequer boards'. Size: 8'6" × 5'0" (facing page), 7'9" × 5'6" (above), 9'6" × 5'6" (right).

Bakhtiari Bakhtiari kilims are woven in double-interlock technique, with cotton warps and wool wefts (above). They are usually long and narrow, with a grid of boxes in the field, or a pattern of boteh or lozenge shapes surrounded by several concentric borders. Horse covers are woven in soumak technique with compositions of animal motifs and bands of colour. Size: 7'0" × 3'6".

Afghanistan

Balouch Dark colours, small white geometric patterns and details in the texture of the weave are all typical of Balouch kilims. They are usually woven partly in weft-faced patterning and partly in soumak technique, and are often made in two halves sewn together, displaying a wealth of fine detail (above). Soffrai, or meal cloths (left), are often square in shape. Size: 9'0" × 5'4" (above), 3'6" × 3'6" (left).

Qala-i-Nau *Very ornate and finely woven in weft-faced patterning, these kilims are characterized by narrow bands of colour and pattern across the width of the rug. Colours are intense, with small areas of white wool woven into the pattern for contrast. Size: 7'9" × 4'3".*

Balouch The Balouch weave many prayer kilims, often with a very simple mihrab shape, and they also make very finely constructed storage bags, decorated with cowry shells and beads.
Size: 6'0" × 3'0".

Taimani Taimani kilims are usually woven in soumak technique, sometimes incorporating knotted work in the border. They are heavy and durable, often dark in colour, and frequently have motifs similar to those found on Persian knotted carpets, with a surrounding border of small stars.
Size: 5'4" × 3'8".

Mukkur *Woven in slitweave using coarsely spun wool, these long, narrow kilims are bright in colour, with reds, oranges and yellows (above). Strong diagonal patterning is emphasized in white. The end fringes are often elaborate tassels decorated with glass beads and small metal discs.*
Size: 11'9" × 4'0".

Sarmayie *Sarmayie kilims from west Afghanistan are woven in one piece in weft-faced patterning (left). They are unusually large, considering that they are woven on ground looms. The colours are soft browns and yellows, and compositions consist of bands or constellations of diamond motifs. Size: 10'0" × 6'8".*

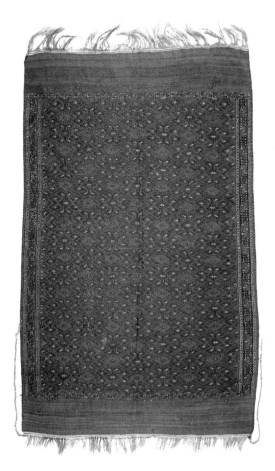

Turkoman Kilims woven by the Turkomen of north *Afghanistan* and *Soviet Central Asia* are frequently large, about twelve or fourteen feet long. Deep madder red and reddish-brown are the predominant colours, with brocaded guls, distinctive to each tribe, woven in dark blue or black wool. Size: 13'3" × 7'8".

Labijar Labijar kilims are recognized by their two distinctively different patterns. Large kilims are woven in a square grid composition of madder red and dark blue squares, with a striking gold double headed arrow motif in each box (left). The other common motif, often used on smaller kilims, is the interlocking 'Christmas tree' design (above). Size: 14'9" × 5'6" (left), 7'0" × 4'0" (above).

Sar-i-Pul These unusual kilims have large areas of white or ivory coloured wool, with small dashes of red and blue woven into the field. Tightly patterned bands of colour in diamond and zig-zag motifs run across the width of the rug at the ends. They are usually long and narrow.
Size: 14′0″ × 5′7″.

Maimana This town is the centre of a prolific weaving area in north-west Afghanistan. Woven in slitweave or dovetailing, the kilims (above and left) are recognized by their strong diagonal patterns made up of small triangles or squares, usually with wide side borders of different running motifs. The colours are bright reds, yellows, oranges and blues, and sizes vary from small doormat size to some of the largest kilims woven. Size: 13′2″ × 6′9″ (left), 6′0″ × 3′0″ (above).

Tartari The distinctive feature of Tartari kilims is the repeated eight-legged 'spider' motif in the field, and a zig-zag border pattern. The colours are madder red, yellows and blues, and the proportions are usually long and narrow. Size: 14'0" × 5'0".

Uzbek The traditional Uzbek kilim is called a 'ghujeri'. Woven in brightly coloured strips of intricate warp-faced patterning, the kilim is sewn together in many different sizes and proportions. The edges are bound with narrow strips of tablet weave or embroidery. Size: 9'0" × 4'6".

Kazakh These extremely heavy soumak kilims are also known as 'Lakai'. The colours are bright red, yellow and orange, with square grid patterns centred by a distinctive gul motif. The sizes vary from a useful hearth rug to large and well proportioned soumak. Size: 8'0" × 6'0".

Details of Weaving Techniques

Plainweave (right) The even, canvas-like texture of a section of plainweave, the simplest weaving technique.

Dovetailing (far right) Simple interlocking technique on a Qashqai kilim.

Double-interlock Detail (right) and reverse (far right) of the double-interlock technique, on a Tartari kilim from Afghanistan. The ridges formed along the back of the weave are clearly visible, as are the firm texture and tight interlocking of colour areas.

Weft-faced patterning (right) The intricate horizontal patterns achieved with weft-faced patterning, on an Afghan Balouch kilim.

Weft-faced patterning (far right) The reverse of the same panel of weaving, showing the 'floating' wefts.

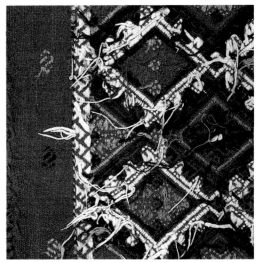
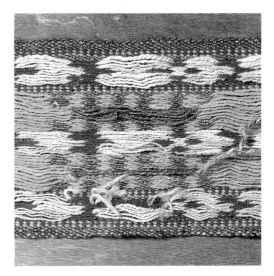

Cicim Detail and reverse of a section of cicim weaving, from a kilim woven in Mut, in Anatolia.

Soumak and zilli Details of the complex soumak (right) and zilli (far right) techniques.

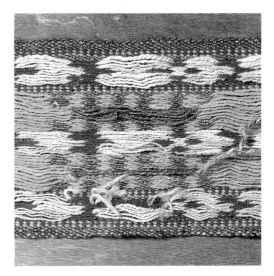

Warp-faced patterning Detail and reverse of a section of warp-faced patterning, on an Uzbek ghujeri from Afghanistan, clearly showing the warps 'floating' along the back of the weave when not in use.

Chapter Four **Kilims on the floor**

Opposite. The colour and pattern of a Tartari kilim from north Afghanistan beautifully reflect the colour and pattern of Victorian tiles. The dramatic zig-zag pattern leads the eye to and from the front door. The kilim must be very hard-wearing to cope with the heavy traffic of feet and dogs, but after five years there is no sign of wear, just some mellowing of colour. A thick felt underlay has been used, helping to soften sounds as well as prolonging the kilim's life.

Kilims on the floor

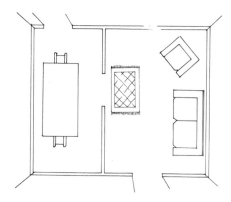

A small kilim adds emphasis to a doorway

MOST KILIMS have been woven over the centuries as ground coverings for tents and houses. Earth floors, mud roofs, courtyards and shaded groves became clean and colourful when arrayed with kilims, and the rituals of welcome, weddings and tribal meetings would then be conducted upon a comfortable scattering of flatweaves. Kilims have traditionally been made to certain specific sizes, determined by their intended use, and by the scale of the loom (and not by the requirements of Western interior designers!) Rectangular kilims are available in all sizes, up to eighteen feet in length and ten feet across, and it is sometimes possible, although much more difficult, to find very large square rugs, or very long, thin runners. Today's Anatolian production has developed and diversified traditional shapes and patterns with Western tastes in mind – indeed, it is possible to commission the weaving of an Anatolian kilim to your own design, so that traditional techniques can be combined with modern, Western needs.

Choosing a kilim to fit a room, or in many cases a room to fit a kilim, will be made a lot easier by following certain functional and decorative principles.

Floor surfaces

Kilims look good on any floor surface, from plain wall-to-wall carpet to polished flagstones, although on certain surfaces an underlay is needed for safety, durability and comfort. Underlay should be cut approximately one inch smaller than the kilim itself. On bare floors, such as stone or wood, underlay will not only prevent the kilim from moving but will also prolong its life, absorbing much of the wear and tear. Kilims are destroyed by the abrasive action of grit and dust which may be ground into the weave underfoot; an underlay will allow these particles to fall through the weave, and not get trapped amongst fibres laid directly onto the floor surface. Underlay will also tend to absorb any minor imperfections in the kilim, such as rucking in the border selvedges, or uneven sections in the weave which might cause it to wrinkle.

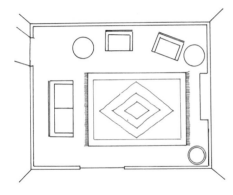

A large kilim laid near the centre of the room. A good floor border is left around it. The central medallion design is not covered by furniture

Tufted pile carpet Kilims laid on top of tufted broadloom fitted carpets tend to 'creep' as they are walked over, and need specialist underlay.
Looped pile carpet This type of carpeting is an ideal surface for kilims, and no underlay will be necessary.
Hessian, sisal and coir matting Underlay is not essential on these surfaces as the kilim will be stabilized on the woven surface of the mat. For comfort, however, and to ease the wear on the kilim, especially with a very rough coir, a thin underlay, such as synthetic felt, should be used.
Wood and tiled floors Kilims on highly polished wood floors and tiled surfaces will slide without underlay. Ordinary felt – or foam rubber-based carpet underlay – can be used to counteract this, and there are specialist kilim underlays, such as sponge and webbing, 'string-vest' types and synthetic felt, available.
Stone floors Unless polished or sealed, stone flags or concrete floors are safe for kilims. On these surfaces the use of underlay will prolong the life of a kilim and add to the comfort underfoot.

Kilim sizes

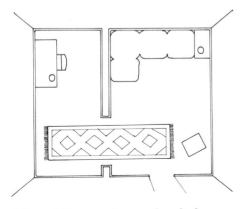

A long kilim can be used to link two adjoining rooms together

The traditional, rather formal, placing of rugs in Western homes (i.e. centrally, leaving a small border of the underlying floor visible) is highly appropriate for kilims; for many people, a kilim is best displayed in the centre of a room or particular space, unhampered by furniture or furnishings, just as a picture is seen on the wall. To achieve this, the kilim should 'float' on the existing surface with a border of at least fifteen inches: very small kilims, of course, require less of this 'floor frame'. Kilims with a central design composition and a formalized border or series of borders are ideal: the existing floor surface then acts as a final outer border or frame.

Less formal decorative effects will be obtained by using a kilim, or many kilims, to break up a room into smaller areas, or to act as a link between rooms that open onto each other. Endless combinations of many different or similarly sized kilims are possible. Fruitless searches for a very wide kilim may be best solved by using two, perhaps runners, placed side by side. The desire to cover a complete floor area with one kilim may also wane in the face of the flexibility achieved by decorating it with many rugs of different sizes. And with an eye to their future use, consider that the same rugs remain endlessly adaptable to other rooms or settings, ensuring the kilims a long and varied decorative life.

Furniture placed on kilims will obviously tend to lessen their decorative effect, especially those with a central design composition, and there is a danger that the weave will be damaged by the movement of chairs, or the sheer bulk of tables and cabinets. Kilims partly hidden by furniture will fade and wear unevenly and should be turned once a year. Underlay and furniture pads or cups should be carefully placed to protect the rug, which should be tightly woven with the minimum of slitweave, since chair legs will tend to catch and rip in the gaps.

Pattern and colour

It is not the size of the kilim that will eventually dominate a room, but the choice of pattern and colour. In general, strong patterns in subtle colours will be easier to place than brightly coloured, eye-dazzling compositions. Kilims with stripes or diagonal patterns and motifs will be less overpowering than strongly centralized designs, and will not need to be placed in the middle of a room or space. Small designs or repeating small motifs may be too fussy or busy for many floors, especially when patterned sofa and curtain materials are used, whereas white walls, the natural grain of wooden floorboards and plain furniture covers are beautifully offset by a blaze of vivacious pattern and colour. Strength of composition and visual subtlety can be achived with a kilim that is woven with two or more scales of pattern. When seen from a distance, these kilims will tend to show their dominant, overall pattern; close to, this strength is dissipated by the other motifs and designs within the composition.

Kilims are available in so many colour combinations that finding an example to match an existing colour scheme is relatively easy. The tone and strength of colour in a kilim can be used to create or add to an impression of visual warmth, or, conversely, to tone down an existing balance or imbalance of colours. Well-lit rooms will be able to accommodate a greater range of colours than dark spaces, and dark floors will tend to enhance a light-coloured kilim. Weaves of totally different patterns, textures and origins will work together in harmony if their colour balance, or their tonal range, are complementary. The variation in the tones of individual colours across the surface of a kilim, caused by using different batches of dyed yarn, is called abrash. Its effects can be subtle or strident, but they do mean that kilims will fit with ease into even the most complicated of colour schemes. There is no substitute, however, for taking home with you a kilim, or preferably a choice of kilims, in order to see their decorative effects on location. It is important to be able to see kilims on trial by natural as well as artificial light, to appreciate their suitability.

Durability

The durability of a kilim when used on the floor is subject to many factors, primarily the structure of the rug – the type of yarn and the weave – and the amount of wear that the kilim is likely to receive, or has received in the past, in the case of an antique or old kilim. A thin, slitweave kilim from Konya in Anatolia will be soft, pliable and less durable than the coarse-textured, stiff and robust, double-interlocked weavings of the Bakhtiari of south-west Persia. Cotton will be less robust than wool or hair from sheep, camels or goats. The tighter the weave and/or the thickness of the construction, the stronger the rug; soumak weaving, for example, produces a very thick fabric. It is well worth comparing the structure of kilims from many different tribes, to get an idea of what will most suit your needs.

Kilims can be used as flooring in two different ways – 'soft' and 'hard' – as determined by the wear and tear to which the rug is likely to be subjected.

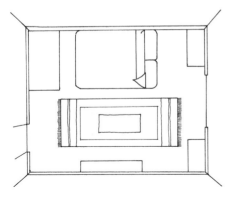

A large kilim alongside the bed. A welcome soft texture for bare feet

Soft use

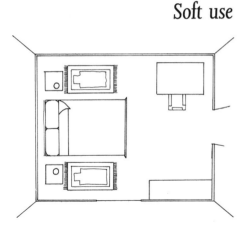

Two small kilims, from a similar area or with matching design, can be fitted on either side of a double bed

Bedroom This is one of the easiest rooms in the house in which to use a kilim, since bedrooms are usually carpeted wall to wall, and there is little hard foot traffic. Small kilims will look good and feel good to step onto when placed by the side of the bed, and the effects of the light from a bedside lamp playing across a favourite kilim are a soothing escape from the pressures of the day before sleep. Pairs of kilims linked by a common design, such as prayer mats or soffrai, are ideal for placing on either side of a free-standing bed: single kilims, especially small runners placed across the foot of a bed, will help prevent the room from being dominated by this single major item of furniture. Bedrooms are often decorated in soft pastel shades, and these can be enhanced by using a kilim of similar colours and subtle patterns. By contrast, a kilim may be chosen to add a focus of strong tribal colours and patterns to the calm of a bedroom.

Bathroom This is an unusual and unlikely room in which to use a kilim, although many small, modern Anatolian and Afghan kilims are almost exactly bathmat size. On a plain carpeted bathroom floor a kilim will add a tough, fairly water-resistant and colourful surface, and on a tiled surface the rug will be warm to walk on, adding a bright focus to the rather stark tiles of many modern bathrooms. A non-slip underlay must be used when a kilim is placed on a tiled surface. Matching the colours and patterns of curtains, blinds, shower curtain, wall tiling and soft furnishings in a bathroom is often very difficult, and a multi-coloured kilim can help to bring cohesion to the overall room design. Kilims used as bathmats should

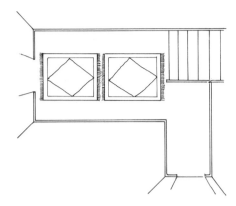

Two matching kilims of a similar size can be rotated to prevent excessive wear on one. The two rugs can visually shorten a long hall

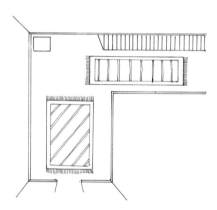

Two kilims laid at right angles will emphasize the irregular shape of the hallway

always be dried after use, and it is best to ensure that the colours are fast.

Study For many the study is a quiet, almost shrine-like room for work and contemplation, where prized, rare kilims, or favourites collected while travelling and full of sentimental value, can be a pleasure to the eye and an aid to thought. The clutter and privacy of a study allows for the use of a profusion of strongly coloured or idiosyncratic rugs, well away from the gaze of visitors and the pressures of fashionable interior design concepts. Choose one rug to fill the entire floor, and cover it with smaller ones dotted about to define particular spaces, or place selected rugs in relation to furnishings and most-used parts of the room. Care should always be taken to ensure that the heaviest and most-moved pieces of furniture in the room, namely the desk and chair, will not damage kilims laid on the floor nearby.

Conservatory Although conservatory floors are invariably hard and cold stone or tiles, the room as a whole is not generally the scene of very heavy through traffic, resulting in comparatively little wear and tear on a kilim. Conservatories are often multi-function rooms that convert from living to dining to play rooms according to changing needs, and so kilims are the ideal floor decorations. They are a warm and decorative floor cover, and they are also light and flexible – easy to fold or roll up and store away when the room is invaded by a children's birthday party.

But there are obvious problems with the use of kilims in the conservatory: floors may be slippery or uneven and damp, and plenty of underlay will be needed. Strong summer light will fade any kilim, and access to the garden will be guaranteed to bring dirt and damp into the room and onto the surface of the rug. Kilims in a conservatory do need to be turned, shaken and cleaned frequently and, if necessary, shades or blinds should be installed to protect the rug from full sunlight.

Hard use

Hallway Size and durability are the most important factors in the choice of kilim for the hall. The hallway offers the visitor his or her first impression of a house, from a corridor with a small, exquisite runner, to a lofty, baronial entrance hall matched by a large dowry kilim. Hallways are often complex in shape, linking the various rooms on the ground floor, and so more than one kilim may be used. Kilims of different patterns, tones or sizes will draw the eye from one separate, clearly defined area to another, whereas kilims that are similar in appearance will tend to link two or more sections of a hallway.

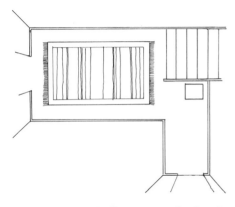

A kilim in the hallway must be hard-wearing, durable, resistant to dirt and laid on an underfelt to prevent sliding. Horizontal bands of pattern can make the hall appear wider

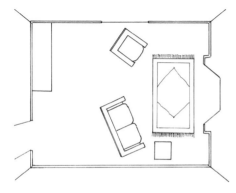

A single kilim laid in front of the fireplace in the traditional manner

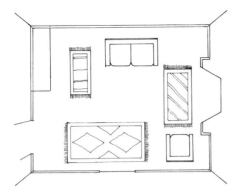

Using a collection of different size kilims in the same room. They can be moved to provide different focuses to areas, or rearranged according to the season

Narrow halls will be given an impression of width by using banded runners with no distinct borders; conversely, an imposing hallway will be made more welcoming by a kilim with strong borders and a central field of multiple and clearly defined designs. Hallways are often not well lit by natural light and so dark kilims will tend to blend in with the gloom, and patterns may become indistinct. In these circumstances, careful artificial lighting comes into its own; the same kilims will glow and come alive when lit with downlighter lamps from the ceiling.

The hall is both entrance and thoroughfare and so any kilims used must be strong and easy to clean. Slitweave kilims are unsuitable for the hall, except for those that are very tightly woven. Densely woven, dark rugs or rugs with small patterns or designs will tend to show the dirt least. Underlay is essential on tiles or wood floors to prevent accidents and to ease the wear on the kilims. Large kilims, although difficult to move, should be lifted and beaten at least once a year.

Living room Living rooms can vary from a central activity area to a quiet drawing room and it is this part of a house that usually embodies a distinct decorative style and on which much money may have been spent. Unless the room may be decorated around a kilim, this is the one position in a house where extreme care must be exercised in the choice of a suitable flatweave floor decoration.

Often the largest room in the house, the living room can take a good-sized kilim that all but covers the floor area. A small kilim will give a focus to one part of the room, such as the fireplace, and a combination of smaller kilims will be more flexible for the arrangement of furniture, and will establish small areas of pattern and colour. Kilims can easily fit into existing colour schemes, and the abrash effect is particularly useful in this respect in a living room, which often contains treasured, but not always perfectly harmonious objects, collected over a period of years. Delicate floral designs will blend more easily than bold geometric patterns, and again, it cannot be emphasized too highly that taking a kilim home on approval is most important; invariably there will be disappointment if a kilim that seemed ideal in a gallery environment looks terrible when placed in the drawing room. Equally, a rug that seemed unremarkable when viewed in a gallery may turn out to be the ideal complement to existing decorations and furnishings when it is taken home and tried out *in situ*. For most living rooms, wear and tear will be less of a consideration than ensuring that a kilim lies flat without creeping; existing floor surfaces are likely to be soft carpeting or hard wood, and so care should be taken to choose the right underlay.

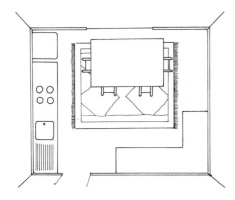

A larger kilim under the table. It must be densely woven and large enough for the chairs to be pulled back without catching on the edge

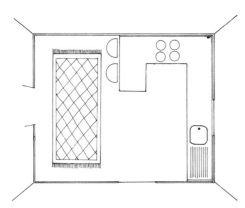

This kilim is laid well away from the busy traffic area by the kitchen sink and cooker. It adds a soft floor cover to the small eating area

Opposite. In the hallway of a home-based art gallery is a bright, busily patterned Mukkur rug. Dense and hard-wearing, with a pattern which does not show dirt and stains, it is a good floor covering for the busy entrance to both house and gallery.

Dining room Kilims may be placed in two distinct areas in a dining room – centrally, under the table, or right away from all movement of chairs and treading of feet. Size and strength should be of primary concern when kilims are used under a table; the kilim should be wide enough to accommodate the movement of chairs without catching the edges too frequently. In order to survive in these conditions, the kilim must be densely woven and not flimsy or too flexible. All but the most tightly woven kilims should be avoided, to prevent the weave from tearing, and colours should be fast so that spills and stains may be removed by cleaning, not damaging the rest of the rug. Formal dining rooms, infrequently used for entertaining, are an ideal situation for kilims; at the other extreme, the kitchen/dining room – always the nerve centre of a house – is one area where a kilim under a table is likely to suffer much abuse.

When a kilim is used under a table, the emphasis of the patterns and colours will be reduced so that matching it to existing decorations will be less of a consideration. A kilim laid away from the seating area will provide an alternative focus to the flat surface of the dining-room table: colours and patterns should complement, repeat or enhance the existing furnishings such as the chair covers and curtains.

Kitchen The kitchen is the utility centre of the home, and will need a robust kilim safely and securely positioned to prevent accidents occurring. Existing floor surfaces are often ceramic, clay, vinyl or cork tiles, flagstones or wooden boards – easy to keep clean and very, very slippery for a kilim; effective underlay is therefore essential and the kilim must lie flat without wrinkles or wavy edges.

The heaviest traffic areas, such as by the sink, work surfaces or kitchen table, are not ideal positions for kilims and a choice of strong or dark colours and busy patterns will show less grime and stains than soft pastels and large designs. A kilim for the kitchen must certainly be hard-wearing and easy to clean.

Playroom A kilim for this children's activity centre must be tough and not too rough or coarse in texture, as children do spend most of their time on the floor. A thick underlay will be comfortable and warm, and colours must be fast so that the inevitable spills and stains may be mopped up without damage to the kilim. Children love to be surrounded by bright colours and vivid patterns, and the strong primaries and bold shapes of many kilims are an excellent stimulus for imaginative games; the kilims can serve as anything from a toy car race-track to a chequer board.

Rich colours and intricate patterns on a long narrow Balouch runner respond beautifully to controlled lighting in a windowless entrance hall in a Belgravia town house in London (left). Horizontal bands across the kilim give the passage an impression of greater width. More complex in shape and lit from north-facing windows, a connecting corridor in an airy Majorca villa (above) has its spaces defined by three smaller kilims with large, bold designs.

The strong black bars on a pair of reproduction Charles Rennie Mackintosh chairs, and on a long Persian runner, lead down a narrow passage to a cleverly placed Balouch kilim indicating the space beyond the arch (right).

Cool marble floors, cascading ferns and a finely woven square Balouch kilim provide relief from the Mediterranean sun, just inside the broad double doors (above).

Oak balustrades gleam around a rectangular Fars rug at the foot of a deep stairwell (right). Bold, white diagonals are seen from the landing, and smaller, more intricate patterns close to.

99

Kilims will blend with any setting. The elegant lines of the multiple arches of an *Anatolian* prayer rug are continued throughout this Manhattan study retreat (above).

Oriental rugs are a familiar sight in the traditional English drawing room, and these *Anatolian* kilims (above) work very well with the peach-brown wall-to-wall carpet. They can be easily moved to vary the decorative effect.

The profusion of colour and pattern in an *Afghan* kilim from Maimana can be dramatically enhanced by plain clay tiles and cream-painted walls in a simply furnished villa (left) or absorbed into the fascinating clutter of a studio living room (opposite).

Beautiful ivory drapes, an antique table and chairs the colour of dark, bitter chocolate are all echoed in the natural wool tones of a Balouch runner, carefully placed to link two full-length windows overlooking the Thames in an elegant first-floor Chelsea drawing room. A similar room in neighbouring Belgravia is treated informally, with a bright blue carpet and two kilims that can be rearranged whenever their owner wants a change of style and emphasis (opposite).

Muted tones of wood, plaster, calico and stone complement the vivid hues of kilims in two newly built homes. In the Mediterranean retreat of a Frankfurt art dealer (left) a large Maimana kilim fills the living room and a smaller Balouch prayer mat provides an intimate focus by the fire.

Glorious late autumn sun, and the colours of the New England Fall, stream in through enormous picture windows, enriching an Anatolian kilim (above); the rug is used to create a small conversation area within a much larger space.

With fine views over the South Downs, bay windows in the drawing room of this English Georgian country house (left) form one side of a delightful seating area, centred around a ghujeri from Uzbekistan.

A cosy sitting room in a country farm house. (above). When the fire is lit in winter, the Persian kilim is saved from sparks and moved to the back of the room.

This huge Sarmayie kilim (left) covers almost the entire floor, leaving a border of stripped pine boards that complement its warm natural colours.

Seating in this open-plan bedroom/office/living room is co-ordinated with a multi-coloured Garmsar kilim (right).

In a modern architect's home (right), zig-zag diagonals and vibrant colours in a large Maimana kilim contrast well with the perpendicular lines of bricks and tiles, chosen carefully to fit the proportions of the sunken seating area.

Tea at sunset in a New York loft apartment with superb views overlooking the Hudson river and the World Trade Center (opposite). Qashqai, Senna and Anatolian kilims are scattered over the polished wooden boards.

With softly gleaming pewter jugs and dark wooden furniture, a quintessentially Flemish interior (above) is completed with an ornate Balouch dowry kilim. Patterns and colours can blend unobtrusively, as in a quiet study (top left), or add a bright, dominant note. An unusual Qashqai kilim brings light and space to the panelled sitting room of a distinguished 1940s New England home (left). Rugs such as this, with large areas of white wool, are very hard to find.

The antiqued, faded colours of an old Persian kilim, with unusual pictorial representations of a man and a woman, and of a goat and a camel, respond well to the soft light from a window in an oak-beamed cottage (below).

Hardwearing kilims can be placed underneath furniture, creating smaller, individual spaces within a room. Chairs, occasional tables and flower decorations surround the glowing fireplace, on an *Afghan Maimana* kilim in a Belgian country-house drawing room (above). A large kilim from the same area is placed beneath the dining table and chairs in a Victorian town house in Belgravia, leaving plenty of room for the movement of chairs, to avoid rucking (right).

Kilims can work well in dimly lit rooms, especially when their colours are as strong and clear as those of the vegetable-dyed Anatolian kilim beneath this dining suite (far right). A Maimana kilim (right) makes the most of daylight across one end of a York-paved room, providing an axis to the much-used shortcut between the kitchen and drawing room.

Set to one side, a strongly patterned kilim can provide a pleasing, alternative focus to the eating area. In this sunny, Long Island house (right) an Uzbek ghujeri is laid across bright, blue-painted boards in a charming, informal dining room.

Children's activities and play usually take place on the floor. In this playroom (opposite), a Garmsar kilim softens and warms the wooden floor, and provides a games board, race track and labyrinth for imaginative stories.

The bed in an apartment overlooking a yacht marina in California (above) is covered with a newly made Usak kilim, and on the floor is another Anatolian piece, a prayer kilim. Kilims will adapt to all kinds of bedroom spaces. A Qazvin kilim from central Persia (right) helps to add colour and pattern to the full-length gallery over the living area – serving as a bedroom – in a Cambridge, England, house.

Opposite. This long runner from north-west Persia is used in an unusual but successful way across the width of the bedroom at the foot of the bed. The warm colouring of the oak panelling, fitted carpet, brass bedstead and patchwork quilt are all picked up in its soft and beautifully aged colours.

A collection of Balouch soffrai runners in a high-timbered bedroom (above). The Persian term soffrai means small rug. These runners, each about 6′0″ × 2′0″, are woven to fill in the edges round the main carpet on a mud floor, in a tent or house.

The floor of this cottage bedroom and bathroom (right) is very uneven, and is covered wall-to-wall with sisal matting. To add softness for bare feet, two square rugs have been put next to the bed and in the bathroom. These square Balouch rugs are rukorsi, traditionally used as a cover for bread ovens to maintain an even temperature.

Under the roof, a combined bedroom, sitting room and work room has a stripped pine floor with a large Caucasian kilim filling the centre of the room (below). The strong top lighting from the roof windows brings out all the colour variation and subtleness in the weave. The geometric pattern and motifs harmonize with the geometric shapes of the chairs and the abstract picture on the wall.

Opposite. A well-lit kilim runner from north-west Persia, carefully chosen to blend the colours with the decor of a bathroom-cum-dressing room.

An ethnic floor covering for the ultra-modern kitchen (above). The Uzbek ghujeri fills the floor space with a narrow border of tiles showing around it.

The axis of a kitchen is turned to a diagonal by the long Anatolian kilim on the floor (above). This rug is well made and lies very flat, an important factor in a room with a lot of traffic.

Cultures meet in a Los Angeles kitchen (right). This very simple striped kilim, woven by the Afghan Balouch, lies on Mexican floor tiles. On the Mexican table is a Burmese puppet, an old man whose role in the theatre is to warm the audience with ribald stories.

A rug from Bergama in west Anatolia provides a soft floor texture in an otherwise very hard room (above). The pattern and colour compete well with the marble tiles.

Christmas in a country conservatory (right). The glowing red and blue squares of a Labijar kilim from Afghanistan add a festive backdrop for the presents and celebrations. Here, on a terracotta floor, the kilim is laid on a felt underlay, and moved, turned or removed to suit the seasonal use of the room.

Chapter Five **Kilims on the wall**

Opposite. The Sivas kilim on the wall, woven by Kurds, is hung from a bamboo pole threaded through a fabric sleeve sewn to the back of the kilim. Many artists and textile designers find inspiration from the patterns and colours found in kilims. In this studio there is a wide choice and the kilims are rotated and changed from a stock kept folded in the chest.

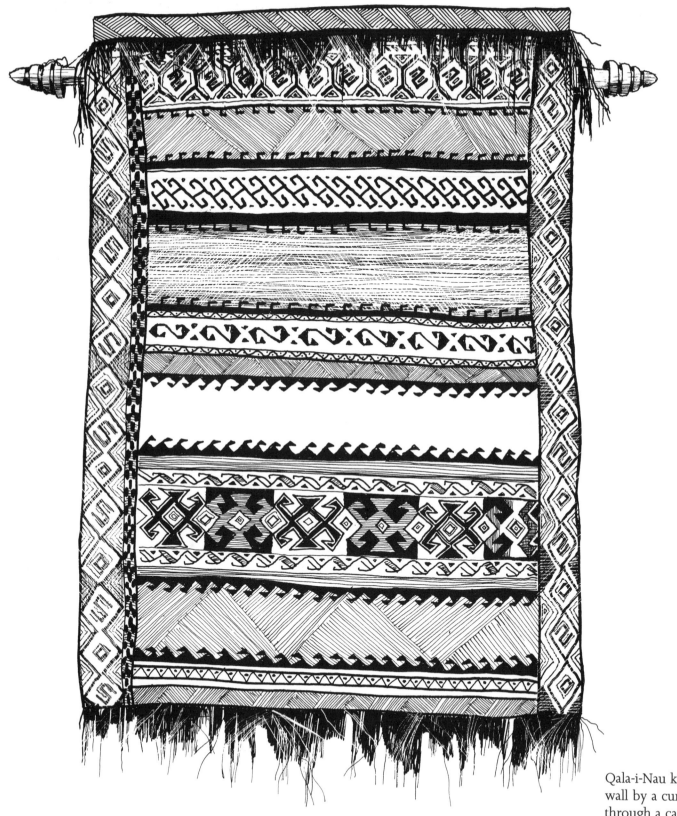

Qala-i-Nau kilim, suspended on the wall by a curtain rail that is threaded through a canvas pocket sewn to the back

Kilims on the wall

Hanging kilims

MOST KILIMS of village or nomadic origin have been made for use on the floor in tents or houses; but there are exceptions, also woven for practical tribal uses. These include tent and mosque doorway hangings, room and tent dividers known as purdah (curtain), and storage bags for clothing, food and utensils that are used to festoon the inside structure of the tents. Many other ordinary floor kilims are seen around the sides of the tent walls, hung as decorations and invaluable as insulation during the winter months.

The kilims and fragments of kilims that have survived from the period of courtly patronage during the Safavid and Ottoman dynasties are so fine and delicate that they must have been made as decorative hangings for the palaces and homes of wealthy princes and merchants. This patronage by the wealthy classes of Persia and Anatolia ended over one hundred years ago, to be replaced by the discerning connoisseur from the West, forming collections of old and fragile kilims that have to be hung on the wall in order to survive intact. The same principle applies to this day, to kilims that have become worn and fragile through long use as rugs, or that are a rare example of their type. They may also be a personal favourite that you wish to protect, or simply suit a certain wall space in a decorative scheme.

Any size and shape of kilim may be hung on the wall, as long as sufficient care is taken to cope with the weight of large flatweaves, and provision is made for the inherent unevenness of their shape. Kilims will look very different when lifted from the floor and positioned on the wall; looking straight at, rather than across a kilim, changes the strength of the composition and colours for the viewer. A 'quiet' kilim on the floor may become a 'loud' and dominating wall hanging, and vice versa. Kilims with a strong focus in the field of one or more designs and a strong border will continually draw the viewer to the centres of those points – a factor which can be both disconcerting and appealing; kilims with a banded or balanced composition will tend to blend and be more relaxing to live with. Prayer kilims are asymmetric and should be hung vertically, with the mihrab

A good place for your favourite, but fragile kilim, is between bookcases in the study

pointing upwards, and some seemingly symmetrical kilims will look quite different when they are turned on end. Similarly, some kilims look better when displayed on the wall in a 'landscape' format, rather than the normal portrait, or vertical format. Experimentation will provide the most decorative solution.

Lighting and the effects of light and heat on kilims hung on the wall are of great significance; strong, natural light streaming onto a kilim will fade the dyes, whether they are chemical or vegetable, and all but the weak morning or evening sunlight will be damaging. Kilims should not be hung over a source of heat, since the drying effects of a radiator or open fire will reduce the natural oil content of the wool, making the weave brittle and the colours dull. Artificial lighting may be used to spotlight a particular section, pattern or motif on a kilim and overall lighting can vary from intense brightness for darker kilims to subtle effects of a brightly coloured one. Shaded table lamps near a kilim on the wall will throw a gentle and diffuse light but any light cast directly across a kilim will show up the texture of the weave, including irregularities of technique or uneven hanging. Sometimes the resultant strong shadows will be effective in highlighting different weaving techniques in the kilim, but they can also detract from the overall power of the composition.

The fabric of the wall and the finish of its surface should be considered when hanging a kilim. Unless you are hoping to hang an extremely heavy kilim on a flimsy partition wall, the fixing of points from which to hang the rug or the frame should not be a problem. Hooks, eyes, screws, staples or nails may be used in conjunction with the relevant hanging technique to suit the nature of the wall, whether timber, hollow framed, stone, brick or metal. There is likely to be a clash of decorative strengths if a kilim is to be hung against a patterned paint or wallpaper surface, and a kilim will certainly look best when offset by a plain painted background, especially white or off-white. Kilims look marvellous in a converted barn, old farmhouse or cottage, hung between the wooden beams against a stone, brick, or painted backdrop, and they are especially easy to hang from the beams of houses with timbered ceilings.

Location and positioning

Alcoves An alcove or an area between wall furniture such as shelving or cabinets is an ideal focus or frame for a kilim on the wall. Cabinets or alcoves with existing hidden pelmet lighting will add a soft glow to the colours and patterns. Small, finely patterned rugs are good for this purpose.

An alcove makes a frame for a bag or prayer kilim hung on the wall

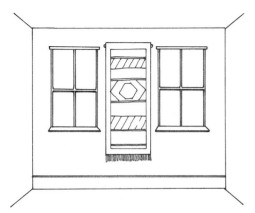

Hung on the wall between two windows, a kilim requires effective artificial lighting to overcome the glare of natural light from outside

Kilims hung on the wall in portrait fashion can foreshorten a long room or hallway. The rugs laid at right angles on the floor indicate there is a further space round the corner

In order to lengthen a space visually, kilims can be hung on their sides

Pictures Kilims may be positioned on a wall in just the same way as a large picture or group of smaller pictures. The kilims will give decorative and personal expression to a setting, and the effect can be dramatic or subtle. A large, centrally patterned kilim hung in isolation and full view will dominate a room or a specific area. A small kilim, carefully chosen, will complement adjacent paintings or textiles, especially when mounted on a frame. It is important to remember that some kilims have two or more scales of patterning. The overall design may be appreciated when viewed from across the room, but smaller details will become apparent at closer range.

Groups A large wall can be divided into smaller areas when decorated with small kilims or bags. Long corridors can be foreshortened by a series of kilims hung to portrait format, and short passageways will be lengthened by kilims hung horizontally, or landscape fashion, stretching into the distance. A collection of unusually shaped weavings such as salt bags or purses can provide an interesting and amusing focus for the kitchen or office, respectively.

Doorways and room dividers Kilims are traditionally hung over doorways, in tent and mosque entrances, and to divide the male and female parts of a tent. Over a door, or *as* a door, a kilim will provide remarkably effective insulation. Kilims hung as room dividers, should, of course, be fully reversible.

Kilims hung on the wall can be used to extend or echo the architectural features of a room, and they do not necessarily have to hang flat. A kilim that splays from a ceiling moulding behind a table to spill onto the floor will seem organic and alive; a similar effect will be achieved when the kilim cascades onto a table or over a chest, emphasizing the textures of the wood and weave. Hanging a rug upon the wall opens up endless new and inventive decorative possibilities.

Methods

Large and heavy kilims should be hung with great care, for it is crucial that the weave, and therefore its weight, be evenly supported along the selvedge or fringe. The kilim should not sag between points of suspension, and single nails or pins, driven through the weave, will eventually tear and weaken the warps and wefts at that point. Fringes should be left to hang over or behind the kilim.

Kilims should not be hung against a wall that is prone to damp, which will rot the wool. Infestations of moth can be prevented by hanging moth balls on the back of the weave on fine threads or by treating the entire hanging with a moth repellent. Moths do not like to be disturbed and so taking a kilim down once or twice a year and giving it a thorough shaking or a light beating will be an effective countermeasure.

Carpet gripper Fitted wall–to–wall carpets are often held in place at the edges of the room by strips of wood faced with small pins, which are then nailed to the floor. This wooden beading, roughly one inch wide and one quarter inch thick, is available in various lengths and is ideal for invisibly supporting kilims on the wall, even though it is known in the trade as 'carpet gripper'. A strip of carpet gripper, one inch shorter overall than the hanging edge of the kilim, should be mounted on the wall with suitable masonry, wood or metal fixings, with the bed of nails pointing outwards from the wall and upwards to the ceiling. The kilim should be centred to the carpet gripper strip and pressed onto the nails, so that it is evenly supported at intervals of about one quarter of an inch. The advantages of this hanging method are manifold; kilims may be easily and repeatedly removed for dusting, cleaning or temporary use on the floor, and small adjustments can easily be made along the row of nails. If a kilim has a tendency to curl at the ends, then small pins, worked through the weave and gently hammered onto the wooden strip, will correct this.

Rod and sleeve Regularly shaped kilims can be hung by sewing a cotton sleeve onto the back, sliding a wood and metal pole through the pocket

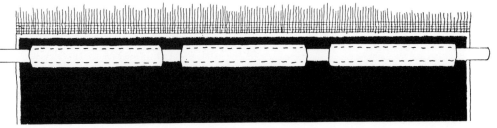

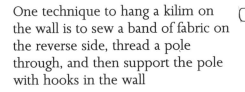

One technique to hang a kilim on the wall is to sew a band of fabric on the reverse side, thread a pole through, and then support the pole with hooks in the wall

and suspending the rod on wall- or ceiling-mounted brackets. A strip of heavy finished cotton, half an inch shorter than the width or length of the rug, and about two inches wide, should be sewn onto the kilim using complementary coloured, fine, but strong cotton thread, about half an inch below the fringe or selvedge. Both edges of this tape should be sewn to the kilim and the ends left open, forming a sleeve through which to pass a wooden or metal pole. The rod itself should be at least two inches wider than the kilim, and should be slid into the eye of a curtain bracket, or left resting on large hooks that have been securely fixed to the wall. A heavy kilim may be supported with the addition of one or more centrally placed wall brackets. It must be stressed that this hanging technique is time-consuming and only suitable for kilims that are evenly made, with straight edges.

Curtain tapes Kilims may be suspended against the wall by sewing a length of curtain tape into and onto the weave, and by attaching small metal rings to the tape that are then hung over a series of picture hooks fitted to the wall. Again, the kilim must be near perfect in shape and weave for the success of this technique.

Wooden beading A lightweight kilim can be stapled or sewn onto a pre-drilled flat wooden pole, cut half an inch shorter than the width or length of the kilim, and suspended from the ceiling or the wall with translucent fishing wire from hooks or eyelets.

Perspex A single sheet of clear or coloured perspex can be used as a mount and frame for a small kilim or kilim fragment. The kilim should be secured to the perspex by sewing thread through the weave and into the hard plastic sheet through a series of pre-drilled holes. The kilim will then appear to float on the surface of the mount and the framing effect may be varied according to the size of the sheet and the colour of perspex used.

A thin kilim or woven fragment will look dramatic when squeezed between two sheets of clear perspex of equal sizes. Brass, chrome or enamelled retaining nuts and bolts at each corner of the perspex should be fixed and tightened onto the enclosed kilim; these may then be extended and located onto the wall or be strung from translucent fishing line or fine and strong metal wire.

Wood or metal frames One of the most elaborate and painstaking methods for hanging kilims involves the construction of a metal or wooden frame over which the kilim may be stretched and secured. In the same manner a backdrop of canvas or self–coloured robust cloth may be stretched over the construction and the kilim can then be sewn, almost embroidered, onto the material. This technique is effective for kilims that are small, lightweight and finely woven.

Opposite. Well lit and carefully hung, kilims of varying origins, from the Bakhtiari of Persia to Anatolian village work, turn the hallway of an eighteenth-century house into an alive, colourful and interesting space.

Above. Hanging over the ancient oak tie beams in the roof space of a sixteenth-century English cottage is a Balouch hurgin, originally used as a saddle pack for a donkey. Over the table is a 1920s quilt from Pennsylvania.

Opposite. An old carved chest from Swat in the North West frontier has been draped by an Anatolian kilim, while a Thracian Tree of Life kilim hangs to the right of a carved house pillar from Nuristan, also in the North West frontier.

Opposite. A prayer kilim is carefully hung as a picture in a small dining room. Close to, the Tree of Life motif is seen in the centre field, while a large-scale pattern in white is apparent when it is viewed from the distance.

The hot, dark red colour of peppers is reflected in an Anatolian bag face (above). Madder red is a frequently used natural dye: the roots of the perennial plant are dried and ground into a powder. The age of the roots, together with the type of mordant, results in a variety of shades and tones from deep purple and rich red to light yellow-red.

Over the fireplace, in a Manhattan town house, a Persian Senna kilim has been hung on carpet gripper (right). The tiny upward pointing pins on the wooden batten, which is fixed to the wall, support the weight of the rug evenly and at many points. The rug may be moved easily for cleaning or adjusting; thus it could be quickly rehung to remove some of the creases.

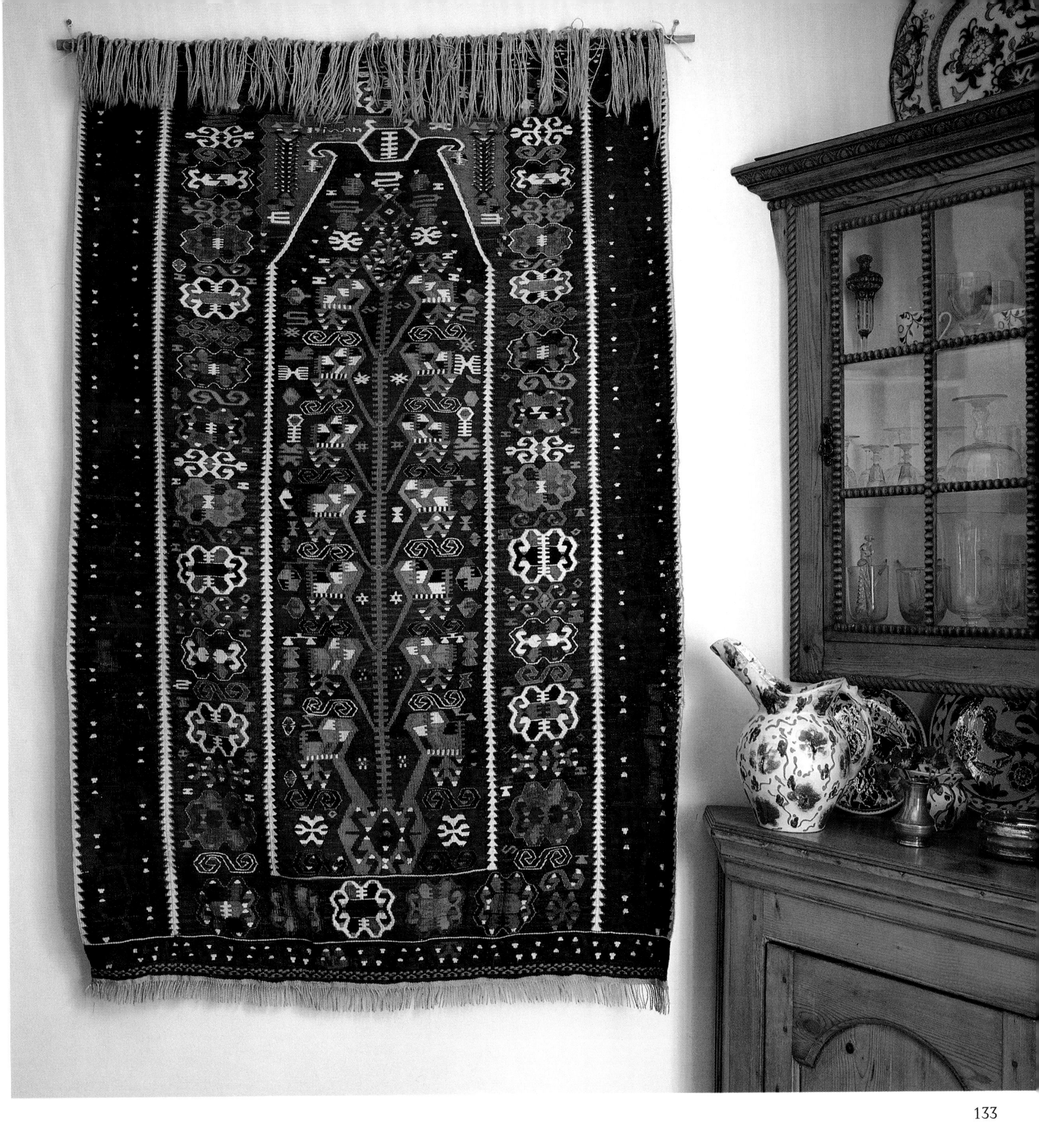

Small tungsten spotlights dramatize the large-scale pattern of this central Anatolian kilim (left). The kilim is fixed to wooden beading behind the pelmet and is displayed in a three-dimensional form as it falls on the floor.

Opposite. Sometimes kilims are too valuable or fragile to be used on the floor. Here a nineteenth-century Sivas/Malatya kilim has seven brass rings sewn to it, and is hung onto hooks fixed to the wall between two alcoves.

The small space on the wall at the top of the stairs is filled by a very finely woven Balouch prayer rug, part knotted carpet and part kilim, woven in the floating weft technique (above). Prayer rugs are very suitable for hanging on the wall because of their small size and the asymmetric pattern of the mihrab design.

In recent years kilims have become an essential item in the designer's palette (opposite). This is an interior designer's studio in a converted sixteenth-century grain store. The kilims are seen as architectural hangings and floor coverings in a set being created for a client. The hanging kilims are recently made Kurdish pieces, with a floral pattern which harks back to the urban weavers of the Safavid dynasty.

In Ghent, Belgium, the Anatolian kilim on the wall of a nun's chapter house reflects the proportions of the door, above which is an unusual bag found by the owner in Malatya and believed to have been used for holding a breadmaker's rolling pin (left).

Opposite. A prayer kilim can be hung on the wall very successfully. The asymmetric design of the mihrab should always be at the top. This rug has been stapled to a wooden batten and hung from eyelets in the beam by translucent fishing line.

In an alcove, beside a Tudor stone fire surround, hangs a bag fragment from eastern Anatolia (above). This carefully lit corner adds a point of interest and colour to the room.

The small Anatolian piece, woven in zilli technique for an unknown but specific function, has been excitingly used as a frame for a wooden crucifix (left).

Opposite. On the angled wall at the end of the gallery, an Anatolian kilim is hung to attract and draw the eye upwards, thereby emphasizing the whole space of the hall. The antique Thracian kilim hanging in Kettles Yard Gallery, Cambridge, England (below), is hung on rings sewn on the reverse of the rug: a cane is threaded through the rings and on hooks set into the wall.

Mixing ideas – and textiles. A director's chair with seat and back from Shahsavan bedding bags, a Bakhtiari clothes bag on the wall, cushions from flatweave fragments and in the distance a tent band hanging (above left). Textiles and rugs from cultures at opposite ends of the world blend together in one room (above). The architect who owns this house (left) has stapled the Malatya kilim to follow the line of the sloping eaves; it hangs down the wall exactly from its centre line.

The antique Senna kilim on the wall (left), made in a town workshop for an urban aristocracy, contrasts well with the simple, colourful pattern of the nomadic kilim on the floor, woven by the Qashqai.

On the wall is a kilim from *Aydin*, in western Anatolia (above). It is hung horizontally across the full width of the wall, with light from the north-facing window streaming across it.

Stables have been cleverly converted into part of an art gallery (right). On the rough brick floor is a tough Qashqai kilim, and on the wall of the stall is a Lakai soumak from Kazakhistan.

Chapter Six **Unusual uses**

Opposite. In this small music room flatweaves have been used for acoustic insulation and decoration, and as a backdrop and frame for a collection of fine violins. On the piano stool, the dense and heavy weave of a Persian bag face makes an ideal cushion.

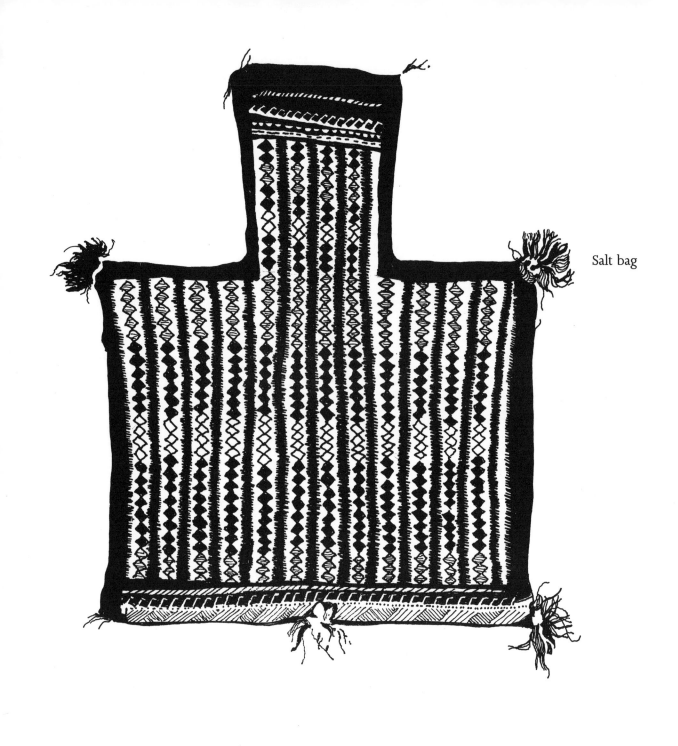

Salt bag

146

Unusual uses

KILIMS are a wonderful way of bringing vibrant colours and patterns to the walls and floors of Western homes: they possess an unusual ability to define spaces, adding warmth and texture, and often provide the essential co-ordinating keynote for an existing decorative scheme. But there is no reason why they should always hang flat, like pictures or tapestries, around the sides of a room, or why they should necessarily lie underfoot, occupying a particular floor space. Lift your kilims up from the floor and down off the wall, and you will find a host of different ways of using them, both practical and decorative; they will soon become an essential part of your household furnishings, and can be used just as flexibly as they are in their countries of origin. Unusual forms such as bags, runners, tent bands and animal covers, as well as straightforward rugs and off-cuts from treasured but well-worn favourites, really come into their own in this way, with a variety of possible uses that are perfectly in tune with Western lifestyles.

Bags In their countries of origin, kilim bags are often made in pairs, and are used for transporting family belongings, either by hand or on the backs of animals, or for hanging as storage around the walls of a house or tent. Kilim-backed carpet bags are stuffed and used as cushions, and very finely woven square bags decorated with tassels are treasured as protective covers for the family Qur'an. Certain forms have evolved for specific purposes, such as namak donneh (square bags with distinctive bottle necks used for storing rock salt), or maffrash (box-like bags sewn together from pieces of kilim fabric, used as bedding sacks). Many of these unusual types can be used in the West, combining decoration, form and function just as successfully as they do throughout the Middle East and Central Asia.

Jaloors and juvals These capacious, heavy flatweave bags are used in their country of origin as panniers for clothing and bedding. When a nomadic tribe is encamped, the bags are hung around the walls of tents; and when the tribe moves on, they are strapped against the flanks of a donkey, ass or camel, laden with clothing and more often than not topped with a small child, lamb or kid. In Western homes such large, colourful and strong hold-alls are always useful, and they can be easily pressed into service as anything from laundry sacks, to bags for children's toys. Stuffed with a very large cushion pad, they also make excellent, hard-wearing and flexible floor seating.

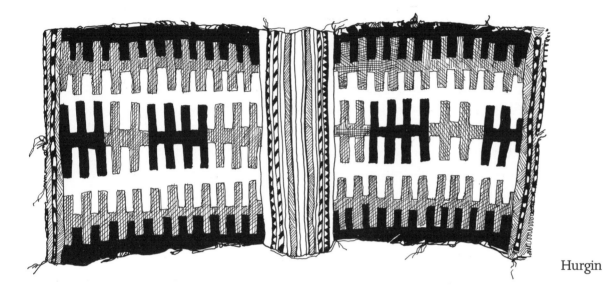

Hurgin

Hurgin These double-sided donkey bags are the original 'panniers', designed to be slung over the back of a domestic animal and used in the kilim-producing areas for carrying provisions and goods for sale. They are frequently used in their countries of origin by tradespeople such as charcoal vendors and onion sellers, as a colourful, eye-catching and strong container in which to transport and display their wares. Smaller hurgin can be slung over the shoulder, and these are often used by shepherds to carry their midday meal and other personal effects. The twin compartments of a hurgin lend themselves to a variety of applications in the West. They can be hung over a bannister and used as a convenient and decorative laundry bag into which the whole family can throw their washing, and they can also be adapted as floor cushions. If each half is stuffed with a large cushion pad, then one part forms the seat, and the other (propped against a wall or frame) acts as the back – a ready-made and very comfortable chair. The effect of a group of such brightly coloured and patterned floor cushions, scattered in a corner, is particularly pleasing and inviting.

Maffrash Nomads and village tribes use these box-like sacks, sewn together from kilim pieces, as storage for bedding. When a tribe is on the move, they are lashed together with leather straps and roped onto a pack animal for transportation. Because of their boxed shape, smaller maffrash make ideal suitcases when modified with strong carrying handles and straps – a durable and attractive alternative to everyday luggage designs.

Purses and vanity bags These smaller flatweave bags are used exactly as their names imply, and can easily be adapted for similar uses in the West. Purses are generally small, narrow and rectangular and can be fitted with a zip to become a tough wallet for keeping cash, chequebooks and credit cards safe. Vanity bags with shoulder straps are, of course, ideal as shopping or book bags, and can also be used as roomy handbags for carrying all kinds of personal clutter such as diaries, purses, pens, notepads, hairbrushes, make-up and so on. It has even been known for two such bags, or a small hurgin, to be adapted as cycle panniers – the ultimate colourful student accessory!

A variety of shapes

Tent bands and runners The absence of ready-made string or ropes in the life of the nomad means that such things have to be woven from strong, pliable yarn in the form of very thin tent bands. These are used for lashing bags to animals as well as for wrapping and reinforcing the barrel-like wooden frame of the nomadic yurt tent, and for securing it to the ground. They are also cut and sewn together to make the rugs known as 'ghujeri'. In Western homes, tent bands make ideal trims along the backs of sofas and chairs, adding a dash of colour, and will make a delicious contrast of tone and texture when placed along the length of a sideboard or console table, protecting and decorating the natural wooden surface. They make attractive wall friezes, and are often used in this way in their countries of origin. Tent bands make a delightful fabric for long mirrors, as well as vibrant pelmet decorations, the perfect complement to plain-coloured drapes. Ideally, one or two long tent bands from the same area of origin should provide enough fabric for a matching set of pelmets and tie-backs, which could even be coordinated with similar furniture trimmings.

'Runner' is a trade term for any long, narrow rug, and such rugs can be used in a variety of ways. Runners may be folded, stitched and stuffed with a long cushion pad to make unusual bolster pillows for beds and sofas, but they are ideally suited for use as staircarpets, enhancing the warm grain of wooden steps, off-set by bright brass stair-rods.

Bakhtiari cradle bag

Square kilims Square kilims are harder to come by than the more common rectangular shapes, but it is possible to find them, and they are often woven in the kilim-producing areas as horse covers or meal cloths. The horse is so highly revered in Anatolia and Central Asia that the woven covers are often beautifully and painstakingly decorated with unusual weaving techniques, using the very finest wool and other precious materials. Indeed, the bridal wedding train of camels and horses is gaily caparisoned with brightly coloured flatweave trappings of all kinds, from jaloors to specially designed collars, knee and harness decorations. Small, square kilims are sometimes used as rolls for carrying laundry to the river, and they are frequently folded to make cradles which are strung like hammocks from the wooden tent frame. Folded corner-to-corner, the cradles are also slung across the back or chest and used as baby carriers by girls and women caring for the youngest members of the family group. Rukorsi kilims, or stove covers, are square rugs placed on top of a pile of felts over the stove, to provide a very warm blanket under the edges of which everyone can huddle in winter.

Because of their shape, small, square kilims lend themselves for use as chair-seat covers and furniture covers, and will, of course, sit evenly on a circular table-top. Kilims are used as meal cloths in Anatolia and Central Asia, and rather than remove the kilim from your table at meal-times, choose an inexpensive, dark-coloured or washable rug as a precaution against staining, or cover it with a smaller cotton cloth when the table is in use. When it is not, the kilim will provide an interesting focus, and an alternative to the often rather plain table surface. Square kilims also make ideal floor cushions if sewn back-to-back and stuffed, or backed with a tough, self-coloured upholstery fabric.

Off-cuts The kilim as a versatile, hard-wearing, canvas-type textile has many uses; brand-new kilims are often cut and made into leather-trimmed handbags or used as upholstery for sofas and foot stools, hassocks, chair seats and backs or padded headboards for beds. Older kilims that have been used on the floor become softer and more flexible over the years, and hence more comfortable to use as a furnishing fabric. A much-loved kilim can be saved from destructive wear and tear on the floor and given a new lease of decorative life if the most worn parts are discarded and the remaining fabric used in this way.

Off-cuts of kilim fabric can be used in a variety of ways. They are ideal for use as upholstery fabric for the seat and back of chairs, and smaller pieces can be sewn into the seams of plain-coloured cushion covers as a strikingly decorative piping. Pieces of fine kilim fabric can be used as anything from book jackets to blinds to patchwork furniture covers, and may be cut and sewn in every way imaginable. Kilims that have seen long service as floor rugs are usually only worn in a few places, leaving plenty of strong, colourful fabric that can be used again.

Decorative furnishings

In their countries of origin kilims are used as insulation and decoration around the walls of a tent or room, and they provide clean, soft flooring, but they are also hung as room dividers and over doorways and can be seen piled on top of chests and slung over furniture as covers, uses for which they are also ideally suited in the West. Kilims used as room dividers should, of course, be fully reversible, as their pattern and design will be displayed from both sides when hanging freely in the middle of a room. Strong wooden beams in a converted barn or cottage are the perfect support for a kilim used in this way; similarly, a strong wooden lintel will provide excellent support for a kilim used as a door hanging, and this can be an ideal way to prevent draughts as well as adding another exciting visual focus.

Sofas may be loosely covered with one large kilim to envelop the whole piece of furniture, or by many smaller, overlapping kilims. Kilims also look effective draped across the back of a sofa, or spread across the seat. Very large kilims will have to be found to make complete sets of fitted sofa and chair covers; a compromise will be achieved by using more than one kilim from the same area of origin, with similar patterns and colours. Weavings used in this way can be cleverly manipulated to enhance or reduce the effect of an unusually shaped piece of furniture. Chests, cabinets and small tables can be protectively and colourfully swagged with kilims, or topped with piles of folded kilims; for many collectors, this is preferable to stowing away unused rugs out of sight in drawers and cupboards.

The vibrant natural colours of kilims take on a completely new depth and quality when they are seen out of doors, and although Western climes are not always as suited to outdoor living as those in the East, kilims are still invaluable as tough, easily portable and highly decorative outdoor accessories. They can add a delightful splash of colour as picnic rugs or on garden tables, and can be spread out on a patio or paved yard to enliven a potentially dull stone or concrete surface – perfect for outdoor entertaining in the summer months. This is a natural extension of their use in the kilim-producing areas, as vibrant and welcoming mats spread before the tent or house door for an honoured guest.

Some of the first kilims appeared in the West by accident, when they were used by Oriental carpet traders as cheap, throwaway wrapping for bales of imported knotted carpets. Their practicality has never been in doubt, but they certainly deserve, and have since found, much higher recognition than this! They have always been used in their countries of origin in an astonishing variety of ways, and in the true spirit of their making they can still serve Western owners in a delightful blend of decoration and function.

Opposite. The entrance hall of a Mediterranean farmhouse. The table is covered with a bright, colourful Anatolian kilim – bright colours usually look best in strong, clear light.

Kilims out of doors. *A bottle of cold wine and a light picnic after a game of croquet on the lawn in front of an English country house. The kilim has been pulled out and unfolded in a traditional style such as at a celebration or picnic in Central Asia (opposite). A cast iron table is covered with a Balouch eating cloth (top left), while two cushions made from part of a Labijar kilim make comfortable seat backs (top tight). The courtyard in southern Spain (right) is a regularly used space all year round. Plants in clay pots and a fig tree give shade to the ancient oak bench during the day, and a cast iron candelabra gives flickering candlelight at night.*

155

An ancient baker's table from France (above) displays a Rajasthan chapati board, Flemish pewter and a Balouch soffrai with knotted border and flatwoven centre.

Opposite. Anatolia comes to a warm homely kitchen. On the tiled floor, the rose design on a black background is very typical of Karabagh kilims. The kitchen table has been set for an informal dinner party with a Malatya kilim as a tablecloth. The size has to be exactly right, and ease of cleaning is clearly important for both kilims.

Three table coverings. Overlooking the Los Angeles skyline, a strip of *Anatolian* flatweave (left). *A* circular Victorian dining table is covered with a *Balikesir* rug, woven originally as an eating cloth (below). The rug hangs with interesting folds, enhanced by the pink silk undercloth. In a less formal setting, in a sixteenth-century Belgian farmhouse kitchen, the table is covered with a soft, flexible Uzbek *ghujeri* (opposite).

Opposite. A kilim from southern Anatolia hangs over a doorway as a room divider between studio and living room. If the kilim is to be seen from both sides it must be either fully reversible or backed with suitable decorative material.

Above. Fragments of Caucasian soumak provide upholstery for a fire settle, while a Qashqai bedding bag, complete with leather straps, has been fitted over a wooden box to display its unusual three-dimensional shape.

Opposite. The winding stairs of a New York duplex have been covered with two Anatolian kilims separated into four lengths. Kilims are often woven in two halves on narrow looms and then sewn together to make a wide rug. On the polished parquet floor is a Garmsar kilim, with underfelt to stop it sliding. The chairs are covered with fragments of Anatolian kilims.

On the wall (top right), the Caucasian bag face has been sewn to a linen-covered wooden back, then framed and faced with clear perspex. There is a Maimana kilim on the floor and the piping of the sofa cushions is from fragments of flatweave. The large comfortable sofa (right) is covered with an old soft kilim from Sarkoy, Thrace.

The striking 'Christmas tree' pattern on the kilim cushion covers (above) indicates the kilim origin as Labijar in Soviet Central Asia. The Anatolian kilim on the floor has been artificially over-dyed to achieve a particular decorative effect. Using a metal frame, a low seat has been created with padded cushions and a donkey bag (opposite). This hurgin is from Garmsar, north-central Persia. Kilims are adaptable! The Chinese country chair was purchased from the man then sitting on it by the Yangtse river. Behind the Venetian chest is a prayer mat from the Greek Islands.

In Cambridge, England, an undergraduate has adapted a donkey bag into a bicycle pannier for books and folders (above). Traditionally, the bag would have been used for carrying small amounts of produce to market, or for a midday meal whilst shepherding. Hung over the banister outside a teenager's bedroom, a Balouch donkey bag is a convenient place to keep dirty washing (below).

The mirror frame and small shelf (above) have been decorated with an *Afghan Turkoman tent band*. The study of a New York collector (opposite) has a Qashqai kilim on the floor, and a checkerboard rug woven by the same Persian nomads on the sofa. The cushions are made from scraps of damaged kilims, and the Spanish chair has been remade with Caucasian soumak.

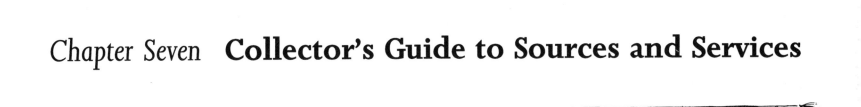

Chapter Seven Collector's Guide to Sources and Services

*Opposite. Rolls and stacks of kilims and cushions
form the stock of a kilim retail business.*

Collector's Guide to Sources and Services

Collecting kilims

UNTIL recently there were, generally speaking, three clear-cut categories from which to choose when buying a kilim; there were antique flatweaves made over 100 years ago, before the influences of export trade began to be felt; there were old kilims, made this century, some of whose compositions clearly display the blending of different tribal and regional traditions; and there were modern, largely commercially produced kilims, woven in village workshops, often to orders from retailers in the West, and often much removed from their local, traditional techniques and patterning.

Over the past five years, however, a fourth category has been added to this list – the new facsimiles being produced in Anatolia. These are completely traditional in style and form, and are made largely as a response to the increasing Western demand for authentic, quality weavings. Many have been specially commissioned by Western dealers, and most are made for export. Various grades are available, determined by the quality of the weaving – from coarse to very fine – and by the complexity of patterning in the overall composition. Most of these kilims are chemically dyed, and those that do make use of vegetable and natural dyes enjoy a considerable premium in price. It is worth noting, however, that chemical dyes have become very much more sophisticated in recent years, and they mimic natural dyes with great success, to the extent that it is often difficult to tell which kind of dye has been used.

The safest purchase in terms of financial investment is, without doubt, an antique kilim. But it is dangerous to assume that a kilim is rare or excellently designed and constructed simply because it is old; there have always been good weavers and bad weavers, weaving good, bad and indifferent kilims. Anyone interested in buying an antique kilim should take time to examine as many old and antique rugs as possible, and should talk to a knowledgeable, trustworthy dealer to get a clear idea of which rugs are considered important and collectable. Collectability is not determined by the vagaries of fashion. A rug is collectable if it is rare or unusual, and if it is very well woven; these are unchanging qualities, and one may assume that such a rug will increase in value as an investment. Antique kilims are invariably the most expensive to buy, both in the West and in their country of origin; ironically, there is often a much better choice in Europe and North America, in terms of price and kilim type, than there is in Anatolia or Central Asia.

Very fine antique kilims are obviously too expensive for many people, but large numbers of old, traditional weavings can be found to suit most budgets. Old kilims are not yet considered a financial investment in themselves, and should really be valued for their decorative and practical qualities on a personal level. Until about thirty years ago, few kilims were produced for commercial gain and so traditional kilim shapes and compositions were made, and weaving techniques practised, as they had been for generations. Antique kilims are now very difficult to find in their countries of origin, and the same will soon be true of traditional old kilims. Their increasing rarity will doubtless be reflected in their rising values.

Of the modern production, it is safe to assume that the finest facsimiles of antique weaving and dyeing techniques will become the investments of the future and the highest quality Anatolian naturally-dyed replicas will definitely improve and mellow with age and use.

Of course, a kilim collection does not have to consist entirely of valuable antiques or museum pieces, and the best 'investments' are often those that most suit your own personal taste and home. With so many recently made kilims available, in such a range of sizes, colours and prices, finding such a rug in the West should be easier now than it has ever been.

Buying For many people, kilims were first seen and collected in Turkey, Central Asia, Iran and Afghanistan. Buying kilims when travelling or on foreign service just before or after the Second World War, when so many antiques and old kilims were readily available, must have been a delightful experience. Turkey is now a very popular and fashionable tourist destination and kilims may still be found both in use and on sale throughout the country. Istanbul still offers the very best and most easily accessible choice of kilims. Do not assume, however, that weavings bought in their country of origin will be cheaper than in the West. A rug bought in a bazaar may often be just as expensive as in London or New York, if not more so. And do beware of the hidden costs and regulations governing a sale for personal export. These include shipping, packing and handling charges, as well as export and import tax. All these expenses add up, and can mean that the overall cost is considerably more than you at first calculate. There is no substitute, however, for the memories and stories associated with the purchase of a kilim in a bazaar: the hours of haggling, the play-acting and the gallons of sweet tea consumed before a deal is struck.

Specialist kilim galleries are a good place to buy rugs in the West. They will have knowledgeable staff and will allow you plenty of time to make your choice, including taking a kilim home on approval. They will also usually have a very good selection of flatweaves; but they can be expensive. Rug galleries are often in glamorous and prestigious locations, with high overheads that can be reflected in their prices. Department stores are now stocking kilims along with knotted rugs in their carpet departments, and these can be cheaper than specialist shops, although you are unlikely to find a large selection of authentic tribal weaves.

Buying a rug at auction in the West can be an enjoyable and nail-biting experience, and there is a great sense of satisfaction in owning a rug for which you have had to compete skilfully. Before you make a serious bid, make sure you are familiar with the current asking price in shops and stores for the kinds of rugs that are being auctioned, and try to go to a couple of auctions without buying, to get a feel for the atmosphere and the procedures involved. Also check whether there are any additions to the hammer price, and make the most of the often limited viewing time before the sale, as rugs bought at auction are not exchangeable if they prove to be unsuitable when you get them home.

Valuation It is important to have a kilim or collection of kilims valued for insurance, buying and selling purposes. This is a very skilled and specialist task, as the correct identification of the source and age of antique or old kilims is, at times, very difficult, and many experts only have a limited field of expertise, confined to one particular area or tribe in the kilim–producing world. Many carpet departments in the auction houses of the world enjoy considerable prestige in their valuation of knotted carpets, but the same cannot always be said, as yet, for their expertise in kilim sourcing and valuing. This same principle applies, in general, to antique dealers, knotted carpet dealers and insurance assessors. If you can ascertain the general area of origin of your rug (see Chapter 3), consult the rug world's two major periodicals, *Hali* and the *Oriental Rug Review*, and use the list of advertisers as a guide to the specialities or particular dealers. From this, and from the list of dealers that follows in this section, you will assuredly find enough brilliant minds to puzzle over your kilim. A complete valuation certificate should include a photograph of the kilim, its dimensions and its source and age. The charge for this service is usually set as a percentage of the valuation.

Selling Advice on where to sell a kilim is much the same as on where to buy. Always go through a trusted dealer or auction house, and note that there are considerable price disparities between countries as well as between auctions on the same site within the space of a year. Consult *Hali* and the *Oriental Rug Review* for prices achieved worldwide in the major auction houses. As with buying, the outcome of selling your rug at auction can be unpredictable, although it is fairly likely that you will do better than by selling to a specialist shop, where the price you receive may be considerably less than the retail price.

Care and repair

Cleaning The everyday care of kilims should include regular vacuuming, preferably not with an upright vacuum cleaner. Take care not to damage the cleaner or the kilim by sucking the fringes into the machine. Kilims will benefit from a vigorous shaking or a good beating, once or twice a year, over a washing line, to remove dust and grit that may have become lodged in the weave. The floor area underneath the kilim should also be vacuumed regularly, and the underlay should be removed and shaken to reduce the likelihood of friction between the weave and particles of dirt.

When washed, kilim dyes are particularly susceptible to running and it is better to have a grubby kilim than one on which colours have run badly, especially from a brightly dyed area onto a white ground. Kilims should only be wet-cleaned after each colour has been tested for fastness. Take a clean, white and very slightly damp cotton rag and gently rub each colour area. If the colour holds fast and does not come off onto the rag, then you can wash the whole kilim, with caution. If any of the colours run, your kilim will have to be cleaned professionally.

Small, colour–fast kilims may be washed in cool water in the bath; larger, and therefore much heavier, kilims should be hosed down on a clean concrete surface and allowed to drip dry on a strong washing line out of direct sunlight. If possible, it is best to dry the kilim stretched out on a board or pegged to the ground, to prevent uneven shrinkage and the subsequent curling corners and corrugations. No detergents should be used and stubborn grime may be teased out with a soft nail brush.

It is also sometimes possible to shampoo a colour–fast kilim with a proprietary foam cleaner such as Novatreat. Using a fairly soft natural bristle brush or a lambswool roller, with a foam cleaner and as little water as possible, vigorously brush each side of the kilim. The resultant foam will evaporate, leaving a white or dirt-coloured dust that may be shaken off or vacuumed. Foam cleaning agents are widely used to clean knotted carpets, and they can remove extremely stubborn stains, but all cleaning solutions should be used with great care on kilims, and manufacturers' instructions should be followed to the letter. It should be noted that some cleaning agents may also bleach out certain colours and dyes.

A natural cleaning solution can be the answer if you are afraid that harsh chemicals might damage your rug, and one such is made from the common herb soapwort. Use one handful of dried soapwort to one gallon of water and boil for one hour. Allow the infusion to cool and then apply as for a chemical cleaner. Difficult greasy stains are best removed with a specialist grease remover, such as Swarfega. Rub a small quantity of the gel into the greasy area and wash out with a little water on a soft brush.

In the event of an accidental spillage, dab the kilim at once with a dry, absorbent cloth and lay newspaper underneath to protect the floor in case any of the colours start to run. If the kilim is colour–fast then it may be cleaned as above, but if colours show any sign of bleaching or running, consult a specialist cleaner.

Repair Minor repairs to kilims can be undertaken by anyone with a strong needle and some matching wool or cotton thread. A simple stitch in time will certainly save the kilim from serious and expensive damage. It is advisable to check the sides and ends of a kilim regularly for signs of wear and tear, or unravelling of the weave for any reason. Kilim ends can be secured with simple blanket stitches and the selvedges can be easily repaired with overstitching in wool or cotton. Specialist wools can be obtained from good embroidery and craft shops, and it is possible to buy both naturally and chemically dyed yarns.

Kilims may develop wrinkles and rucks with use, corners may tend to curl and some never seem to want to lie flat. Stretching and more complicated repairs can often cure this, but it is advisable to leave these to the professionals.

Well-used or old kilims often become brittle and dry out, when the wool loses its essential oils. Rugs that have lost their patina in this way can be restored in a most original manner: lay the kilim out on a level surface and take a large handful of newly shorn and untreated sheep's fleece. Rub the raw wool rhythmically all over both sides of the kilim. This will restore some of the lost lanolin and be excellent exercise!

Further Reading

Magazines *Hali* and the *Oriental Rug Review* are the two main periodicals covering all aspects of the rug world. Both are readily available throughout the UK, US and Europe, and *Hali* publishes a special German-language supplement.

Hali Publications Ltd, Kingsgate House, Kingsgate Place, London NW6 4TA, UK
Tel: 0171 328 9341

Oriental Rug Review, Beech Hill Road, Meredith, NH 03253, USA Tel: 603 279 5574

Books *Afghanistan* Roland Michaud and Sabina Michaud, 1985

The Art of the Felt Maker M.E. Burkett, 1979

The Arts and Crafts of Turkestan Johannes Kalter, 1984

Caravans to Tartary Roland Michaud and Sabina Michaud, 1985

Carpet Magic: the art of carpets from the tents, cottages and workshops of Asia Jon Thompson, 1983

Flat Woven Rugs of the World: Kilim, Soumak, Brocading Valerie S. Justin, 1980

Kilim, Cicim, Zili, Sumak Belkis Balpinar Acar, 1982

Kilims: The Art of Tapestry Weaving in Anatolia, the Caucasus and Persia Yanni Petsopoulos, 1980

The Qashqai of Iran Lois Beck, 1986

Nuristan L. Edelberg and S. Jones, 1979

Oriental Rugs, Part III, 'Carpets of Afghanistan' R.D. Parsons, 1983

Rugs of the Wandering Baluchi David Black, 1976

The Techniques of Rug Weaving P. Collingwood, 1976

Textile and Weaving Structures: a sourcebook for makers and designers P. Collingwood, 1987

Textiles of Baluchistan M.G. Konieczny, 1979

Tribal Rugs: an introduction to the weaving of the tribes of Iran Jenny Housego, 1978

Tulips, Arabesques and Turbans: decorative arts from the Ottoman Empire Yanni Petsopoulos (ed.), 1982

Turkish Flat Weaves: an introduction to the weaving and culture of Anatolia W.T. Ziemba, A. Akatay,
S.L. Schwartz, 1979

The Undiscovered Kilim David Black, 1977

International auction houses

Many auction houses will value and sell kilims, and many have branches in other countries and in provincial towns.

France
Ader Picard Tajan
12 Rue Favart, Paris 75002
Tel: 1 42 61 80 07

Germany
Ketterer
Brienner Strasse 25, D – 8000 Munich 2
Tel: 89 591181

Rippon Boswell
Friedrichstrasse 45, D – 6200 Wiesbaden
Tel: 6121 372062

Switzerland
Galerie Koller
Ramistrasse 8, 8024 Zurich
Tel: 1 475040

Ineichen
C.F. Meyerstrasse 14, 8002 Zurich
Tel: 1 2013017

United Kingdom
Christie's
8 King St., St. James's, London SW1Y 6QT
Tel: 0171 839 9060

Phillips
7 Blenheim St., London W1Y OAS
Tel: 0171 629 6602

Sotheby's
34/35 New Bond St., London W1A 2AA
Tel: 0171 493 8080

United States of America
Butterfield and Butterfield
220 San Bruno Avenue, San Francisco
CA 94103
Tel: 415 861 7500

Christie's East
219 East 67th St, New York, NY 10021
Tel: 212 606 0400

Grogan & Company
890 Commonwealth Avenue, Boston
MA 02215
Tel: 617 266 4200

Phillips
406 East 79th St, New York, NY 10021
Tel: 212 570 4830

Robert W. Skinner
Route 117, Boston, MA 01451
Tel: 617 779 5528

Sotheby's
1334 York Avenue, New York, NY 10021
Tel: 2123 606 7000

Opposite. Kilims are not afraid of the late twentieth century. A very beautiful and rare antique southeast Anatolian prayer kilim is laid at the double doors to a postmodern dining room.

Opposite. A collection of salt bags grouped together on a white painted brick wall makes an interesting feature of shape and texture. Salt bags are distinguished by the narrow neck to the bag, folded down to keep the precious salt dry.

Using the unusual. Creating a focus around the seating area with a Kuba kilim laid on the blue-painted, boarded floors (above).

Doorways don't have to be avoided (right). The door swings well above the Anatolian rug and will not damage it.

Thinking about purpose. A formal Chelsea apartment, overlooking the River Thames, suggests a rug that is imaginative in composition and not too tribal in colour or pattern (above). The kilim is the full width of the hall and is laid on cream-coloured hessian. On the highly polished floor under the leather couch is a kilim from north-west Persia (opposite). The horizontal band pattern is frequently found in kilims from this area, and is successfully used in the well-composed, minimalist corner of this New York living room.

Responding to – and creating – an atmosphere. A room for contemplation, reading and study (below). Good lighting brings out the strength of patterning in these two kilims, both from Persia and both of a size frequently woven, 11'0" × 5'6". Living and kitchen areas are linked by a Malatya kilim (opposite).

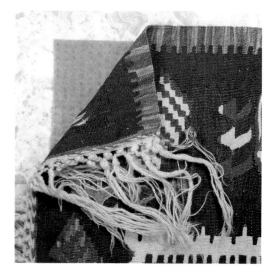

Underlay. Top, l. to r. *Synthetic webbing (for hard or slippery floors); sponge and webbing (hard); synthetic felt (hard). Above. String-vest type (for carpets: available in another quality for hard and slippery). Repairing a kilim (right). The leading edge of the warps to the finish of the pattern is being replaced. Tools of the repair business: pliers, needles, staples, wool, pins. The kilims in the background are waiting to have small holes and damaged areas repaired.*

Dealers, sources and services

In this section, the names and addresses of dealers from all over the world are listed, together with the services they offer (e.g. cleaning and repairing) and the kinds of artifacts stocked. Obviously it is not possible to list everybody, but we have tried to give details of well-established houses and traders, as well as some more unusual and specialist galleries and businesses. It is advisable to call before you visit a dealer or showroom – some are only available by appointment, and it is always worth checking opening times.

Key to services and types of artifacts stocked:

Imp.	Importer	A.	Antique
Ret.	Retailer	O.	Old
W.	Wholesaler	N.	New
Manu.	Manufacturer		
Col.	Collector		
Rep.	Repairs		

N Af.	North Africa	Pers.	Persia/Iran
Anat.	Anatolia	Afgh.	Afghanistan
Cauc.	Caucasus		

Australia

Nazar Rug Galleries Pty Ltd,
583 Military Road,
Mosman,
New South Wales 2088
Tel: 2 969 2659/331 1505
Imp., Ret., W., Rep.; A., O., N.;
Anat., Cauc., Pers., Afgh.
A well-established business that does expert repairs and valuations.

Austria

Ali Aslani,
Genupft Garten (Woven Garden),
Salesianergasse 23,
A-1030 Vienna
Tel: 1 713 9734
Imp., Ret., W.; A., O., N.; Pers.

Adil Besim,
Stammhaus, Graben 30,
A-1014 Vienna
Tel: 1 533 0910
Imp., Ret.; A., O., N.

Herbert Bieler,
Erlaufstrasse 25/8,
A-2344 Ma. Enzerdorf
Tel: 2236 26986

Hannes Boesch,
Hans Sachs Gasse 7,

A-8010 Graz
Tel: 316 78730
Ret., Rep.; A., O.; Anat., Cauc., Pers., Afgh.

Galerie Safor,
Naglergasse 29,
A-1010 Vienna
Tel: 1 533 3289
Ret., W.; A., O.; Anat., Cauc., Pers.
Outstanding and antique carpets and kilims.

Galerie Sailer,
Wiener Philharmonikergasse 3,
A-5020 Salzburg
Tel: 662 846483
Imp., Ret., Rep.; A.; World

Kelimhaus Johannik,
Krugerstrasse 10,
A-1010 Vienna
Tel: 1 512 4287

M. Kirdok,
Seilerstatte 19,
A-1010 Vienna
Tel: 1 513 9394

Bernhard Voloder,
Steingasse 35,
A-5020 Salzburg
Imp., Ret.; A., O.

Beate von Harten,
Burggasse 24/12,
A-1070 Vienna
Tel: 1 933 0493
Manu., Rep.; A., O.
A high standard of restoration work carried out with selected materials and colours.

Belgium

Kailash Gallery,
Komedieplaats 7-9-11,
B-2000 Antwerp
Tel: 3 231 92 46

Geert Keppens,
Ruilare 54,
B-9130 Zeveneken, Lokeren
Tel: 91 55 96 17
Fax: 91 55 28 97
Imp., Ret., W., Rep.; A., O.;
Anat., Cauc., Pers., Afgh.
A frequent and experienced traveller in Anatolia, Iran and Afghanistan; buyer of unusual kilims, knotted carpets and ethnographica.

Etienne Roland,
Noville Les Bois,
B-5380 Fernelmont

Tel: 81 83 40 05
Fax: 81 83 46 20
Imp., W.; A., O.; Anat., Cauc., Pers.
Open by appointment. Selection for the interior decorator and antique dealer. Makes kilim cushions and furniture.
Herman Vermeulen,
Kraanlei 3,
B-9000 Ghent
Tel: 91 24 38 34
Imp., Ret., W.; Rep.; A., O.;
Anat., Cauc., Pers.
A stock of over 500 kilims is always held, and these include old decorative examples, new, naturally dyed kilims and a large selection of 19th century and earlier flatweaves. More than eighteen years' buying experience in the Middle East.

Canada

El Pipil Crafts,
267 Danforth Ave.,
Toronto, Ontario M4K 1N2
Tel: 416 465 9625
Ret.; O., N.

Kilim Crafts,
401 Richmond St West,
Suite 358,
Toronto, Ontario M5V 1X3
Tel: 416 593 7126
Ret.; A., O., N.

The Oriental Carpet Store,
55 York St,
Stratford, Ontario N5A 1A1
Tel: 519 273 3207

Rubaiyat Craft Gallery,
722 17th Ave. South West,
Calgary, Alberta T2S OB7
Tel: 403 228 7192
Fax: 403 245 2727

Sharanel Inc.,
Toronto, Ontario
Tel: 905 509 4423
Fax: 905 509 4424
Imp., W., Col.; A., O., N.; Pers., Afgh.
Open by appointment. Owner Geoff Somes travels regularly to Afghanistan and Iran in search of kilims, kilim bags, tent bands, *soufreh* and related kilim accessories.

Unicorn for Fabulous Gifts,
HWY 6, Morrison,
Ontario, N0B 2CO
Tel: 519 767 1553

Vernacular,
1166 Yonge Street,
Toronto, Ontario M4W 2L9
Tel: 416 961 6490
Fax: 416 961 7730
Ret.; A., O., N.; Anat., Pers., Afgh.
A gallery specializing in the tribal arts.

The Wheat Sheaf,
R.R.2,
Milford, Ontario K0K 2PO
Tel: 613 476 7730
Old and new kilims, bags, etc.

Woven Gardens,
816 Rue Ouimet,
P.O. Box 1769,
St Jovite, Quebec J0T 2HO
Tel: 819 425 8491
Ret.; O., N.
A wide selection of floor coverings, kilims, ethnic and antique artifacts.

Denmark

Wiinstedt Orientapper,
Stranboulevarden 9,
Copenhagen 2100
Tel: 31 38 78 19

France

Apamée,
3 Rue Maître Albert,
75005 Paris
Tel: 1 46 34 04 40
Imp., Ret.; A.; Anat., Cauc., Pers., Afgh.
Antique kilims and carpets.

L'Art Turkmene,
26 Rue Auguste Comte,
69002 Lyons
Tel: 78 38 21 54
Imp., Ret., W., Rep.; A., O.;
Anat., Pers., Afgh.

Galerie AK Kurt,
72 Rue du Cherche-Midi,
75006 Paris
Tel: 1 42 22 10 49
Imp., Ret.; O., N.; Anat., Pers.
The owners visit Turkey each year to buy kilims, carpets and textiles.

Galerie Triff,
35 Rue Jacob,
75006 Paris
Tel: 1 42 60 22 60
Ret.; A., O.; Anat., Cauc., Pers.

Germany

Galerie Neiriz Berlin,
Kurfürstendamm 175,
D-1000 Berlin 15
Tel: 30 882 3232
Imp., Ret., W., Rep.; A.; Anat.,
Cauc., Pers.
A private kilim collector who
sells antique pieces in four exhi-
bitions each year.

Galerie Ostler,
Ludwigstrasse 11,
D-8000 Munich 22
Tel: 89 285 669
Ret.; A.; Anat., Pers.
Their focus is weaving as
an art form.

Eberhardt Herrmann,
Theatinerstrasse 42,
D-8000 Munich 2
Tel: 89 293 402

Kokon,
Esslingerstrasse 14,
D-70182 Stuttgart
Tel: 711 233 416
Graf Toerringstrasse 13,
D-8229 Seefeld
Tel: 81 52 7722
Mashallah!,
Schellingstrasse 52,
D-80799 Munich 40
Tel: 89 272 3623
Imp., Ret.; A., O., N.; Anat.,
Pers., Afgh.
Handmade textile home furnish-
ings, as well as a variety of tribal
decorative arts from all over the
world.

Krausse,
Maximiliansplatz 15,
D-8000 Munich 2
Tel: 89 294 838

Mohammed Tehrani,
Auf dem Sande 2,
D-2000 Hamburg 11
Tel: 40 367 587
Fax: 40 374 3306
Imp., W.; A.,O.; Anat., Pers.,
Afgh.
Nomadic and tribal rugs, kilims
and small weavings a speciality.

Holland

D.W. Kinebanian,
Heiligeweg 35,
Amsterdam
Tel: 20 26 70 19
Ret., W.; A., O.; Anat., Cauc.,
Pers., Afgh.

Traditional family business specializing in antique and old
kilims and carpets.

Ireland

Peter Linden,
10 Rock Hill,
Main Street,
Blackrock,
Dublin
Tel: 3531 885 875

Italy

The Carpet Studio,
Via Monalda 15/R,
50123 Florence
Tel: 55 21 14 23
Ret.; A.; Mostly Anat.
Primarily specializes in antique
carpets and textiles, but does
have a small selection of kilims.

Luciano Coen,
Via Margutta 65,
00187 Rome
Tel: 6 678 32 35/679 03 21
Ret.; A.; Anat., Cauc., Pers.
Stocks a few and very selected
antique kilims. His Swiss wife
speaks fluent English and
German.

Eskenazi,
15 Via Montenapoleone,
20121 Milan
Tel: 2 76 00 00 22
Ret.; A., O.; Anat., Cauc., Pers.
For the last twenty years, have
specialized in old and antique
weavings; organizing two exhibitions ('Kilim', 1980, and 'Anatolian Kilims', 1984), with cata-
logues. Have also published a
book in four volumes on kilims:
The Goddess from Anatolia, Balpinar,
Hirsch and Mellaart (1989).

Ghalibaf,
Corso Vittorio Emanuele 40,
Turin
Tel: 11 87 80 93/87 23 86
Via Cavour 19,
Alessandria
Tel: 131 55 688
Piaza San Secondo 15,
Asti
Tel: 141 54 730
Oriental Textile Studio,
Via Cavour 17, 1st Floor,
Turin
Tel: 11 43 60 065
Ret., Rep.; A., O., N.; Anat.,
Cauc., Pers.

A large choice of antique and
prestigious carpets and kilims.

Kilim Arte & Antichita,
Via Fama 15,
37121 Verona
Ret.; A., O.
Kilims and textiles.

The Kilim Gallery,
Via di Panico 8,
00186 Rome
Tel: 6 68 68 963
Imp., Ret.; A., O., N.; Anat.,
Cauc., Pers.
Kilim specialist.

Il Mercante D'Oriente,
Corso S. Anastasia 34,
37121 Verona
Tel: 45 59 41 52
Ret.; Rep.; A., O., N.; Anat.,
Cauc., Pers.
Buys and sells tribal and village
textiles.

Daniele Sevi,
6 Via Fiori Chiari,
20121 Milan
Tel and Fax: 2 87 61 69
Ret.; A., O.
Specializes in rare Oriental
carpets and flatweaves.

Dario Valcarenghi,
6 Via F. Corridoni,
Milan
Tel: 2 54 83 811
Imp., Ret., W.; A., O.; Anat.
A large collection of antique
and old kilims.

New Zealand

Robert Buchanan,
36 Garfield Avenue,
P.O. Box 5489,
Dunedin
Tel and Fax: 34 67 25 01
Imp., Ret.; A., O., N.; Anat.,
Oriental
Importer and retailer of old and
new rugs, kilims and textiles.
Direct importer of kilims and vil-
lage rugs, plus a small selection
of old shawls, textiles and
copperware.

Portugal

De Natura,
162a Rua da Rosa,
1200 Lisbon
Tel: 1 34 66 081
Imp., Ret.; A., O., N.; N Af.,
Anat., Afgh.

Handicrafts and articles for interior decoration.

Spain

Puerto Galera,
Dr Roux, 30 Torre,
Barcelona 17
Tel: 3 2 05 05 12

Sweden

J.P. Willborg,
Sybyllegatan 41,
114 42 Stockholm
Tel: 8 783 0265/0365
Imp., Ret., W., Rep.; A.; Anat.,
Cauc., Pers.
Antique textile gallery.

Switzerland

Djahan Orientteppiche,
Freilagerstrasse 47,
Zollfreilager,
CH-8043 Zurich
Tel: 1 491 9797
Imp., W.; A., O., N.; Anat.,
Cauc., Pers.
A well-established firm
renowned for their great collec-
tion of kilims.

Galerie Kistler Dekor KI AG,
Bernstrasse 11,
CH-3250 Lyss
Tel: 32 84 44 33
Imp., Ret., W.; A., O.; Anat.,
Cauc., Pers., Afgh.
Nomadic art gallery.

Graf & Raaflaub AG/Ltd,
Rheingasse 31/33,
CH-4005 Basle
Tel: 61 25 33 40
Imp., Ret., Rep.; A.; Anat.,
Cauc., Pers.

Theo Haeberli,
Lindenstrasse,
CH-9062 Lustmühle
Tel: 71 33 29 55

Nomadenschätze,
Weyrmuhle,
5630 Muri/AG
Tel: 57 44 42 18
Kirchgasse 36,
CH-8001 Zurich,
Tel: 1 252 5500
Imp., Ret.; A., O.; Anat., Pers.,
Afgh.
Tribal flatweaves, rugs, textiles
and jewelry.

Jurg Rageth,
Sieglinweg 10,
Riehem,
CH-4125 Basle
Tel: 61 67 33 22
Imp., Ret., W.; A., O.; Anat.
A well-known kilim specialist
with a wonderful collection of
interesting kilims.

Ali Shirazi,
Zollfreilager Block 1,
Kabin 337,
Postfach 159,
CH-8043 Zurich
Tel: 1 493 1108
Imp., W.; A., O.; Pers., Afgh.
A collection of unusual nomadic
pieces.

Teppich Stettler AG,
Amthausgasse 1,
CH-3011 Berne
Tel: 31 21 03 33
Imp., Ret., Rep.; O., N.; Anat.,
Cauc., Pers., Afgh.
An enterprise specializing in
nomadic and cottage rugs,
kilims and bags.

Zollanvari,
Freilagerstrasse 47,
Block 4 5th floor,
CH-8043 Zurich
P.O. Box 156
Tel: 1 493 28 29
Fax: 1 493 07 73

UK

Aaron Gallery,
34 Bruton Street,
London W1X 7DD
Tel: 0171 499 9434/5
Imp., Ret., W.; A., O., N.
Islamic and ancient art.

Ananda,
19 Bond Street,
Brighton BN1 1RD
Tel: 01273 607 772
Ret.; O., N.; Anat., Pers., Afgh.

J.L. Arditti,
88 Bargates,
Christchurch,
Dorset BH23 1QP
Tel: 01202 485 414
Ret., Rep.; A., O., N.; Anat.,
Cauc., Pers.
Old Oriental rugs, runners and
kilims bought and sold. Cleaning
and restoration service.

Axia Gallery,
43 Pembridge Villas,

London W11
Tel: 0171 727 9724

Nathan Azizollahoff,
Oriental Carpet Centre,
Top Floor, Bldg. A,
105 Eade Road
London N4 1TJ
Tel: 0181 802 0077
Imp., W.; O.; Anat., Pers., Afgh.
Established in London in 1921, a
customs-bonded warehouse han-
dling Oriental carpets and textiles
old and new. Good selection of
large and unusual sizes.

Sara & David Bamford,
The Workhouse,
Presteigne Industrial Estate,
Presteigne,
Powys, LD8 2UF
Tel: 01544 267 849
Restoration and conservation
specialists.

Bernadout & Bernadout
7 Thurloe Place,
London SW7 2RX
Tel: 0171 584 7658
Antique and semi-antique Orien-
tal carpets and rugs.

David Black Oriental Carpets,
96 Portland Road,
Holland Park,
London W11 4LN
Tel: 0171 727 2566
Fax: 0171 229 4599
Ret., Rep.; A., N.; Anat., Cauc.,
Pers.
Established for 26 years. Has
published a wide range of books
and mounted several major exhibitions. Mainly deals in antique
weavings but also carries a stock
of new, naturally dyed kilims
and rugs from the Dobag project
in western Turkey.

Cargo,
23 Market Place,
Cirencester,
Gloucestershire
Tel: 01285 652175

Chandni Chowk,
1 Harlequins,
Paul Street,
Exeter,
Devon EX4 3TT
Tel: 01392 4\0 201
Imp., Ret., Col., W.; A., O., N.;
N Af., Anat., Pers., Afgh.
Wide range of new, old and
antique folk and tribal applied
arts.

Coats Oriental Carpets,
4 Kensington Church Walk,
London W8 4NB
Tel: 0171 937 0983
Ret., Rep.; A.; Anat., Cauc.,
Pers., Afgh.
Antique collector's pieces.

Eastern Artifacts,
42/43 Royal Park Terrace,
Edinburgh EH8 8JA
Tel: 0131 652 1962
Imp., Ret., W.; O., N.; Afgh.
Tribal rugs, kilims, cushions and
bags of the Balouch, Turkomen,
Uzbeks, Tartari, Taimani and
others. By appointment.

Christopher Farr Handmade
Rugs,
115 Regents Park Road,
Primrose Hill,
London NW1 8UR
Tel: 0171 916 7690
Ret., Rep.; A., O., N.; Anat.,
Pers. A pioneering gallery
devoted to the best antique and
new rugs, kilims and textiles
from the Near East.

Galerie Mirages,
46a Raeburn Place,
Edinburgh EH4 1HL
Tel: 0131 315 2603
Imp., Ret.; O., N.; Anat., Afgh.
Gallery specializing in ethnic art.
Permanent collection of kilims
on display, but also holds special
exhibitions.

Graham & Green Ltd.,
4 Elgin Crescent,
London W11 2JA
Tel: 0171 727 4594
Imp., Ret.; O.; Mainly Anat.
Specializes in furniture, kilims,
fabrics and decorative accessories, offering an updated approach
to traditional English furnishing.
Kilims carefully chosen for their
decorative and useful qualities.

Joss Graham,
10 Eccleston Street,
London SW1W 9LT
Tel: 0171 730 4370
Ret., Rep.; A., O.
Well-established business specializing in tribal and ethnic textiles
of all kinds, including many
types of kilim weaving.

J.P.J. Homer,
Stoneleigh,
Parabola Road,
Cheltenham,

Gloucester GL50 3BD
Tel: 01242 234 243
Ret., Rep.; A., O.; Pers.
Sale and repair of antique rugs,
saddle bags, runners and occasio-
nally kilims.

Alastair Hull,
The Old Mill (correspondence)
or 18A High Street (gallery)
Haddenham,
Ely, Cambridge CB6 3TA
Tel: 01353 740 577
Fax: 01353 740 688
Imp., Ret., W.; O., N.; Pers.,
Afgh.
Travels frequently to Afghanistan
and Iran, buying kilims to sell
from his gallery and from exhi-
bitions in unusual venues around
the UK.

The Kilim & Nomadic Rug
Gallery,
5 Shepherds Walk,
London NW3 5UE
Tel: 0171 435 8972
Ret., Rep.; A., O.; Anat., Pers.
Dealer travels extensively around
Anatolia seeking old and unusual
kilims.

The Kilim Warehouse Ltd,
28A Pickets Street,
London SW12 8QB
Tel: 0181 675 3122
Fax: 0181 675 8494
Imp., Ret., W., Rep.; A., O., N.;
Anat., Cauc., Pers., Afgh.
Founded by José Luczyc-
Wyhowska in 1982. A well-
known importer of kilims, with
an interesting warehouse in an
unusual location.

Alison Kingsbury,
No 1 Lodge,
Great Hampden,
Great Missenden,
Bucks HP16 9RD
Tel: 01494 488571
Repairs carried out personally by
an experienced and trained
weaver.

Christopher Legge Oriental
Carpets,
25 Oakthorpe Road,
Summertown,
Oxford OX2 7BD
Tel: 01865 57572
Imp., Ret., W., Rep.; A., O., N.;
Anat., Pers., Afgh.
Buyers and sellers of all types of
Oriental rugs, also offering valua-
tion and cleaning services.

Liberty Retail Ltd,
Regent Street,
London W1R 6AH
Tel: 0171 734 1234
Ret., O., N.; N Af., Anat., Pers.,
Afgh.
Carpet department has a large
kilim business, showing good-
quality, interesting old and new
rugs, saddle bags and horse
covers.

Clive Loveless,
29 Kelfield Gardens,
London W10 6NA
Tel: 0181 969 5831

Martin & Frost,
130 McDonald Road,
Edinburgh EH7 4HN
Tel: 0131 557 8787
Ret., Rep.; O., N.; Anat., Afgh.
Quality home furnishings with a
specialist Oriental rug and carpet
department. Knowledgeable staff.

Moroccan Rugs & Weavings,
5a Calabria Road,
London N5 1JB
Tel: 0171 226 7908
Imp.; A., O., N.; N Af.
Open by appointment. 5-day
exhibitions twice a year.

Garry Muse,
26 Mostyn Gardens,
London NW10
Tel: 0181 969 5460
Ret.; A.; Anat.
Rare Anatolian kilims and rugs.

Odiham Gallery,
78 High Street,
Odiham,
Hampshire RG25 1LN
Tel: 01256 703415
Imp., Ret., Rep.; A., O., N.;
Anat., Cauc., Pers., Afgh.
Specializes in rugs and kilims for
interiors. An emphasis on colour
and design as opposed to rarity.

Oriental Rug Gallery,
42 Verulam Road,
St Albans,
Herts AL3 4DQ
Tel: 01727 41046
Imp., Ret., W., Rep.; O.,
N.; Anat., Pers., Afgh.
Specializes in quality kilims with
furnishing colours bought dir-
ectly, cleaned and restored.
Approximately 200 weavings
always in stock, including bags
and tapestries of very large sizes.
Trial-at-home service available.

Orientis,
Digby Road,
Sherborne,
Dorset DT9 3NL
Tel: 01935 816 479/813 274
Ret., Col., Rep.; A., O., N.;
N Af., Anat., Pers., Afgh.
Deals in antique textiles and
Oriental rugs; a cleaning and
repair service is also available.

Out of the Nomad's Tent,
21 St Leonards Lane,
Edinburgh EH8 9SH
Tel: 0131 662 1612
Fax: 0131 667 6107
Imp., Ret., W.; A., O., N.;
Anat., Iraq., Pers., Afgh.
Owner Rufus Reade collects most
kilims at source, travelling
widely to find interesting exam-
ples. Selling exhibitions are held
all over the UK.

The Read Molteno Gallery,
Nomads House,
High Street,
Stockbridge,
Hampshire SO20 6HE
Tel: 01264 810 888
Fax: 01264 810 481
Ret.; O., N.; Anat., Pers., Afgh.
Specializes in ethnic decorative
artifacts including kilims,
textiles, carvings, furniture and
jewelry.

Gordon Reece Gallery,
Finkle Street,
Knaresborough,
Yorkshire HG5 8AA
Tel: 01423 866 219/866 502
Imp., Ret., W., Rep.; A., O.;
Anat., Cauc., Pers., Afgh.
A permanent stock of over 1000
rugs, mostly of Persian origin.
Organizes two specialist exhibi-
tions per season.

Graeme Renton Orientals,
72 South Street,
St Andrews,
Fife KY16 9JT
Tel: 01334 76334

Clive Rogers Oriental Rugs,
22 Brunswick Road,
Hove,
Brighton,
Sussex BN3 1DG
Tel: 01273 738 257
Imp.; A., O., N.
Oriental carpets and kilims.

Samarkand Galleries,
2 Brewery Yard,

Sheep Street,
Stow-on-the-Wold,
Gloucestershire
Tel: 01451 832322

Robert Stephenson,
1 Elystan Street,
Chelsea Green,
London SW3 3NT
Tel: 0171 584 8724/225 2343
Imp., Ret., Manu.; A., O., N.;
Anat., Cauc., Pers.
A wide range of decorative flat-
weaves stocked, including Eas-
tern European rugs. Kilim-
covered furniture a speciality.

Thames Carpet Cleaners,
48–56 Reading Road,
Henley-on-Thames,
Oxfordshire RG9 1AG
Tel: 01491 574 676

Dennis Woodman,
105 North Road,
Kew,
Surrey TW9 4HJ
Tel: 0181 878 8182
Ret.; O., N.; Anat., Pers., Afgh.
An interesting gallery displaying
rugs, kilims and textiles.

USA

Adraskand Inc.,
15 Ross Avenue,
San Anselmo, CA 94960
Tel: 415 459 1711
Ret., W.; A.; Anat., Cauc., Pers.,
Afgh.
Sales and exhibitions of antique
tribal and village rugs, kilims and
textiles. Stocks new, but traditionally designed and made, Anatolian kilims.

Anahita Gallery,
P.O. Box 1305,
Santa Monica, CA 90406
Tel: 213 455 2310
Fax: 213 455 2490
Imp.; A., O.; Afgh.
Open by appointment. Specia-
lizes in ancient and ethnic art of
Central Asia, including rugs,
textiles, jewelry and decorative
and architectural wood.

Michael Andrews Antique Orien-
tal Rugs,
2301 Bay Street 302,
San Francisco, CA 94123
Tel: 415 931 5088
Ret., W.; Anat., Pers.
Open by appointment.

Antique Carpet Gallery,
533 S.E. Grand Avenue
Portland, OR 97214
Tel: 503 234 1345
Ret., W., Rep.; A., O.; World
A gallery specializing in old and
antique pieces, with an emphasis
on natural dyes and good
condition.

Ariana Rug Gallery,
411 King Street,
Alexandria, VA 22314
Tel: 703 683 3206
Ret., W.; A., O., N.; Anat., Afgh.
Specializing in Afghan weavings,
both kilims and knotted carpets.

Asia Minor Carpets,
801 Lexington Avenue,
New York, NY 10021
Tel: 212 223 2288
Fax: 212 888 8624
Imp., Ret., W., Manu., Col.,
Rep.; A., O., N.; Anat.
Carries a full line of Turkish antique and old kilims and carpets,
as well as vegetable dyes and
100% hand-spun wool kilims
and carpets with traditional
designs produced in their workshops in Turkey. Specializes only
in Turkish goods.

J.R. Azizollahoff,
303 Fifth Avenue, Suite 701,
New York, NY 10016
Tel: 212 689 5396
Ret., W., Col.; A., O., N.; Anat.
Open by appointment. Specializes mostly in natural dyed Turkish carpets and kilims. New and
antique carpet consultant for
designers and private buyers.

Berbere Imports,
144 South Robertson Boulevard,
Los Angeles, CA 90048
Tel: 213 274 7064
Imp., Ret., W., Rep.; A., O., N.;
Anat., Cauc., Pers., Afgh.
Importers of rugs and kilims that
are distinguished by truly ethnic
design, colour and weave, and
large size.

James Blackmon Gallery,
2140 Bush Street #1,
San Francisco, CA 94115
Tel: 415 922 1859
Fax: 415 922 0406
Imp., Ret., Rep.; A.; Anat., Pers.
Appraises, lectures on, cleans,
conserves and sells antique
textiles.

Dennis R. Dodds/Maqam,
19 West 55th Street, Suite 6A
New York, NY 10019
Tel: 212 977 3603
Fax: 212 977 5814
Ret., Col.; A.; Anat., Cauc., Pers.
Specializes in unusual and rare kilims, tribal rugs and antique textiles.

Miranda E. Dupuy,
236 W. 10th Street #19,
New York, NY 10014
Tel: 212 255 6280
Rep.
Private textile conservator specializing in kilims and other flatweaves. Rugs and trappings restored for utilitarian purposes or conserved and prepared for display.

George Fine,
One Cottage Street,
Easthampton, MA 01207
Tel: 413 527 8527
Imp., Ret.; A., O.; Anat.
Travels in Anatolia, collecting kilims for designers, retailers and collectors.

Foothill Oriental Rugs,
1464 Foothill Drive,
Salt Lake City, UT 84108
Tel: 801 582 3500
Imp., Ret., W., Rep.; A., O., N.;
Anat., Cauc., Pers., Afgh.
A comprehensive selection from all major rug-producing countries except China. Specializes in flatweaves and tribal rugs.

Fortunate Discoveries,
1730 West Wrightwood,
Chicago IL 60614
Tel: 312 404 0212
By appointment.

Hazara Gallery,
6251 College Avenue,
Oakland, California
Tel: 510 655 3511
Ret.; A., O.; Anat., Cauc., Pers.,
Afgh.
Specializes in tribal weavings such as carpets, kilims, embroideries and trappings.

Kilim,
150 Thompson Street,
New York, NY 10012
Tel: 212 533 1677
Imp., Ret.; A., O.; Anat., Cauc.,
Pers.
Specializes in old and antique kilims, saddle bags, prayer

kilims, runners and tribal kilims in all sizes.

Krikor Markarian,
151 West 30th Street, Room 801,
New York, NY 10001
Tel: 212 629 8683
W. Rep.; A., O.; Anat., Cauc.,
Pers.
Small and room-size antique, collectable rugs and kilims. Restoration and hand-cleaning service.

Le Souk Gallery,
1001 East Alameda,
Santa Fe, NM 87501
Tel: 505 989 8765
Imp., Ret.; A., O.; N Af.
Open by appointment. Berber arts a speciality.

Marian Miller Kilims,
148 East 28th Street, 3rd Floor,
New York, NY 10016
Tel: 212 685 7746
Imp., Ret., W.; A., O., N.; Anat.,
Cauc., Pers.
Old and antique kilims, with a selection of new Anatolian kilims.

Stephen A. Miller Oriental Rugs Inc.,
212 Galisteo Street,
Santa Fe, NM 87501
Tel: 505 983 8231
Ret., Rep.; A., O., N.; Anat.,
Cauc., Pers., Afgh.
Comprehensive selection in all sizes, representing major weaving centres of the world.

Nomad,
279 Newbury Street,
Boston, MA 02116
Tel: 617 267 9677
Ret.; O.; Afgh.
International folk and tribal art gallery.

O'Bannon Oriental Carpets,
5666 Northumberland Street,
Pittsburgh, PA 15217
Tel: 412 422 0300
Ret., Rep.; A., O., N.; Anat.,
Cauc., Pers., Afgh.
A retail carpet shop specializing in Turkish village rugs, kilims and utilitarian objects.

Obatu-Afshar Inc.,
311 West Superior, Suite 309,
Chicago, IL 60610
Tel: 312 943 1189
Ret.; A., O.; Pers.

A kilim gallery specializing in antique and old flatweaves from Persia.

James Opie Oriental Rugs Inc.,
214 SW Stark Street,
Portland, Oregon, OR 97204
Tel: 503 226 0116
Ret.; A.; Pers.
Weavings and kilims from southern Iran have long been the speciality of this store.

The Pillowry L.A.,
8687 Melrose Avenue,
G770 West Hollywood,
CA 90069

The Pillowry N.Y.,
132 East 61st Street,
New York, NY 10021
Tel: 212 308 1630
Fax: 212 996 2836
Imp., Ret., W., Col., Rep.; A., O.
A world-wide collection of antique and old textiles, including kilims and trappings. Specialists in work on upholstery, hassocks and pillows.

The Rug Collector's Gallery,
2460 Fairmont Boulevard,
Cleveland Heights, OH 44106
Tel: 216 721 9333
Ret.; A., O.; Anat., Cauc., Pers.,
Afgh.
Specialists in fine, old and antique rugs and kilims of artistic merit.

Sakrisabz,
Penn's Market, Rt 202,
Old York Road Store, No 20,
Lahaska, Pennsylvania
Tel: 215 794 3050
Imp., Ret., W.; A.; Afgh.
Direct importers of antique kilims, textiles, brasswork and carvings from Central Asia.

Shaver Ramsey Oriental Galleries,
2414 East Third Avenue,
Denver, CO 80206
Tel: 303 320 6363
Imp., Ret.; A., O., N.; Anat.,
Pers., Afgh.
A vast collection of kilims, from antique, classic and collectable, to the more modern and decorative.

Mark Shilen Gallery,
109 Greene Street,
New York, NY 10012
Tel: 212 925 3394
Ret.; A., O.; Anat., Pers., Afgh.

All types of tribal weavings, with a strong emphasis on kilims.

Silk Route Corp,
3119 Fillmore Street,
San Francisco, CA 94123
Tel: 415 563 4936
Imp., Ret., W., Manu., Col.,
Rep.; A., O., N.;
N Af., Anat., Cauc., Pers., Afgh.
More than 35 years of experience in the rug business, both in the USA and Afghanistan.

Sümer Nomadic Rugs,
P.O. Box 587,
Hardeeville, SC 29927
Imp., W.; Anat., Cauc.

Sun Bow Trading Co.,
108 Fourth Street NE,
Charlottesville, VA 22901
Tel: 804 293 8821
Imp., Ret., W., Rep.; Anat., Pers.,
Afgh.
Source acquisition of tribal and nomadic textiles and rugs from Konya to Kashgar.

Tamor Shah,
3219 Cains Hill Place NE,
Atlanta, GA 30305
Tel: 404 261 7259
Imp., Ret., W.; A., O.; Afgh.
Fine antique and semi-antique rugs, kilims, tapestries, embroideries, costume and lace.

Trocadero Textile & Nomadic Art,
2313 Calvert Street at Connecticut Avenue NW,
Washington, DC 20008
Tel: 202 328 8440
Imp., Ret., W., Col., Rep.; A., O.,
N.; Anat., Cauc., Pers., Afgh.
A well-established firm renowned for their great collection of antique kilims, tribal weavings and ethnographic furniture from the Swat Valley and Morocco. Exceptional repair service available on rugs and textiles. Pillows, kilims and carpet bags are available.

Turkana Gallery,
125 Cedar Street, Penthouse,
New York, NY 10006
Tel: 212 732 0273/
516 725 4645
Imp., Ret., Rep.; A., O.; World
Open by appointment. Primarily a kilim dealer.

Woven Legends Inc.,
922 Pine Street,
Philadelphia, PA 19107
Tel: 215 922 7509
Imp., Ret., W., Rep.; A., O., N.;
Anat., Cauc., Pers.
A constantly changing selection
of fine antique and modern
kilims.

International kilim collections

There are many museums and galleries worldwide with famous, rare and important kilims among their carpet collections. Those listed here are all accessible to the public, but some can only be viewed by appointment.

Austria

Museum of Applied Art,
Stubenring 5,
A - 1010 Vienna

Ethnological Museum,
Ringstrassentrakt, Neue Burg,
1014 Vienna

Germany

Islamische Museum,
Staatliche Museen zu Berlin,
102, Bodestrasse 1/3, Berlin

Kestner-Museum,
Trammplatz 3, Hanover

Museum für Islamische Kunst,
Staatliche Museen
Preussischer Kulturbesitz,
Stauffenbergstrasse 41,
Berlin 30

Turkey

Mevlana Museum, Konya

Bursa Turkish and Islamic Art
Museum, Bursa

United Kingdom

Fitzwilliam Museum,
Trumpington Street,
Cambridge CB2 1RB

Horniman Museum
and Library,
London Road, Forest Hill,
London SE23 3PQ

Museum of Mankind,
Burlington Gardens,
London W1

Pitt Rivers Museum,
South Parks Road,
Oxford, OX1 3PP

Victoria and Albert Museum,
Cromwell Road, London SW7

United States of America

Boston Museum of Fine Arts,
Boston, MA 02115

William Hayes Fogg
Art Museum,
Harvard University,
Cambridge, MA 02138

Metropolitan Museum of Art,
Fifth Avenue, New York,
NY 10028

Textile Museum,
2320 S. Street N.W.,
Washington, D.C. 20008

Kilims illustrated in the colour photographs on location

p.17 *N.W. Persia* (bottom) 7'4" × 4'0"
N.W. Persia (centre) 8'3" × 4'0"
Lakai (centre left) 2'0" × 2'0"
p.18 *Balouch* 4'9" × 4'3"
p.19 (top) *Maimana* (bottom)
17'0" × 7'0"
Balouch (left of bed) 5'6" × 3'3"
p.19 (bottom right) *Turkoman* (curtains) (fragment)
p.19 (bottom left) *Senna* (left)
5'0" × 3'6"
Tartari (right) 2'3" × 2'3"
p.20 *Bakhtiari* (on table) 5'6" × 3'3"
pp.20–1 *Yoruk* (centre) 6'6" × 3'9"
Yoruk (centre) 4'7" × 3'4"
Balouch (left) 4'0" × 2'6"
Van (right) 4'6" × 3'4"
p.22 *Veramin* 10'0" × 6'6"
p.23 (top left) *Anatolia* 12'0" × 2'6"
p.23 (top right) *Garmsar* 11'0" × 5'0"
p.23 (bottom) *Manastir* 5'0" × 3'0"
p.24 *Qazvin* 14'0" × 3'3"
p.88 *Tartari* 14'0" × 6'6"
p.97 *Mukkur* 12'0" × 5'0"
p.98 (left) *Balouch* 9'3" × 2'6"
p.98 (right) *Malatya* (top) 8'0" × 4'8"
Aydin (centre) 5'3" × 3'6"
N.W. Persia (bottom) 9'0" × 4'0"
p.99 (top left) *Balouch* 4'0" × 4'0"
p.99 (top right) *Balouch* (top)
4'0" × 4'0"
Kurdish (bottom) 8'0" × 2'0"
p.99 (bottom) *Fars* 4'6" × 3'6"

p.100 (top left) *Central Anatolia*
10'6" × 5'0"
p.100 (top right) *Sivas* (centre)
7'6" × 4'6"
Konya (bottom) 6'0" × 3'0"
p.100 (bottom) *Maimana* 15'9" × 9'0"
p.101 *Maimana* 13'0" × 6'0"
p.102 *Balouch* 5'9" × 2'3"
p.103 *Balouch* (centre) 6'9" × 2'9"
Sarmayie (bottom) 8'0" × 3'5"
pp.104–5 *Maimana* (bottom)
13'3" × 6'9"
Balouch (fireplace) 5'0" × 3'0"
p.105 *Karabagh* 9'0" × 5'0"
p.106 (top left) *Uzbek* 10'0" × 5'6"
p.106 (bottom left) *Sarmayie*
14'9" × 8'0"
pp. 106–7 *S. Persia* 9'6" × 4'9"
p.107 (top right) *Garmsar*
13'6" × 6'6"
p.107 (bottom right) *Maimana*
12'6" × 7'0"
p.108 (top left) *Manastir* 5'0" × 3'0"
p.108 (bottom left) *Quashqai*
8'0" × 4'6"
p.108 (centre right) *Balouch*
10'0" × 4'6"
p.109 *Senna* (centre left) 6'6" × 4'0"
Anatolia (centre right) 5'6" × 4'0"
Quashqai (bottom) 11'0" × 4'6"
p.110 (top left) *Maimana*
15'0" × 10'0"
p.110 (bottom left) *Maimana*
11'6" × 6'6"
pp.110–11 *Bijar* 14'0" × 4'0"
p.111 (top centre) *Maimana*
7'6" × 4'0"
p.111 (top right) *E. Anatolia*
11'5" × 6'5"
p.111 (bottom right) *Uzbek*
8'6" × 4'6"
p.112 *Garmsar* 10'6" × 6'0"
p.113 (left) *Usak* (bed) 9'10" × 7'3"
Obruk (floor) 5'0" × 3'8"
p.113 (right) *Qazvin* 9'9" × 4'6"
p.114 (top) *Balouch* 6'0" × 2'0" each
p.114 (bottom) *Balouch* (top)
3'8" × 3'10"
Balouch (bottom) 3'6" × 3'6"
p.115 *Bijar* 14'6" × 2'9"
p.116 *Shirvan* 12'9" × 6'9"
p.117 *Zarand* 9'0" × 3'6"
p.118 (top left) *Sivas* 15'7" × 5'0"
p.118 (top right) *Uzbek* 5'2" × 4'3"
p.118 (bottom) *Balouch* 13'0" × 4'6"
p.119 (left) *Bergama* 5'9" × 4'0"
p.119 (right) *Labijar* 12'0" × 5'0"
p.120 *Sivas* (wall) 5'3" × 3'6"
Shirvan (floor) 11'0" × 5'8"
p.129 *Qashqai* (wall, left) 9'0" × 5'0"
Malatya (wall, centre) 9'9" × 5'4"
Sivas/Malatya (floor)
p.130 *Balouch* 2'6" × 2'6"
p.131 *Central Anatolia* (chest)
12'0" × 6'6"
Thrace (wall) 7'6" × 4'6"
p.132 (left) *Anatolian bag face*
p.132 (right) *Senna* 6'0" × 3'6"
p.133 *C. Anatolia* 5'7" × 4'0"
p.134 *Konya* 12'6" × 4'0"
p.135 *Sivas/Malatya* 12'9" × 6'2"
p.136 *Balouch* 4'9" × 2'9"
pp.136–7 *Kurdish* 6'6" × 3'6"
Kurdish 5'4" × 3'3"
p.138 (top left) *Yoruk* (right)
5'0" × 3'0"
Malatya (bag)
p.138 (centre) *E. Anatolia* 3'6" × 2'0"

p.138 (bottom left) *Obruk* 2'9" × 2'9"
p.139 *Erzurum* (wall) 6'0" × 3'0"
Labijar (floor) 11'0" × 6'0"
p.140 *Sivas/Malatya* 4'6" × 3'0"
p.141 *Thrace* 9'0" × 5'0"
p.142 (bottom left) *Malatya*
12'0" × 6'0"
p.142 (top left) *Bakhtiari clothes roll*
p.142 (top right) *Shahsavan* (wall)
7'6" × 3'6"
Shirvan (centre) 8'0" × 5'0"
Qashqai (bottom) 10'0" × 5'0"
p.143 (left) *Aydin* (wall) 13'9" × 3'9"
Qashqai (floor) 3'9" × 3'9"
p.143 (centre top) *Senna* (wall)
6'6" × 4'6"
Qashqai (floor) 8'5" × 4'5"
p.143 (bottom right) *Lakai* (wall)
7'3" × 3'6"
Qashqai (floor) 7'9" × 3'9"
p.144 *Kurdish bag face*
p.153 *Malatya* 8'3" × 4'8"
p.154 *Maimana* 13'2" × 6'9"
p.155 (top left) *Balouch* 4'0" × 4'0"
p.155 (top right) *Labijar* (fragments)
p.155 (bottom) *Labijar* 6'3" × 3'9"
pp.156–7 *Malatya* (tablecloth)
8'3" × 4'10"
Karabagh (floor) 7'7" × 4'9"
p.157 *Balouch* 3'9" × 3'9"
p.158 (left) *Central Anatolia*
p.158 (right) *Balikesir* 4'3" × 4'0"
p.159 *Uzbek* 9'0" × 7'0"
pp.160–1 *S. Anatolia* 6'6" × 3'6"
p.161 *Qashqai bedding bag*
p.162 *Anatolia* (stairs)
Garmsar (floor) 8'5" × 4'5"
p.163 (top) *Caucasian bag face* (wall)
Maimana (floor)
p.163 (bottom) *Sarkoy* 12'6" × 11'3"
p.164 *Van* 6'4" × 5'9"
p.165 *Garmsar hurgin*
p.166 (centre top) *Balouch hurgin*
p.166 (bottom left) *Balouch hurgin*
p.166 (right) *Turkoman tent band*
p.167 *Qashqai* (sofa)
Qashqai (floor) 9'0" × 5'0"
p.168 *Aydin* (wall, l. to r.)
Garmsar, Kurdish, Shirvan (floor, l. to
r.) *Qashqai, Aydin*
p.177 *S.E. Anatolia* 5'0" × 2'0"
p.178 (left) *Kuba* 9'6" × 5'0"
p.178 (right) *Anatolia* 12'0" × 5'0"
p.179 *Balouch salt bags*
p.180 *Karabagh* 11'6" × 5'6"
p.181 *N.W. Persia* 13'6" × 4'6"
p.182 *Garmsar* 11'0" × 5'6"
p.183 *Malatya* 9'0" × 2'6"

Index

Page numbers in italics refer
to illustration captions

abrash 92, 95
Achaemenidae 58
Aegean 54
Afghanistan 16, 28, 29, 30,
    38, 40, 44, 50, 60, 62, 171;
    61, 68; kilims 15, 28, 29,
    40, 47, 48, 49, 61–4, 93;
    18, 19, 62, 155; people 15,
    61–4; *66*
Aimaq 62, 63, 64
alcove 124; *20, 125, 134, 138*
Alexander 61
Anatolia 12, 16, 30, 31, 34,
    38, 41, 44, 46, 48, 50, 149;
    51; kilims 28, 31, 35, 39,
    40, 48, 49, 50, 51–6, 90,
    93, 150, 170, 171; *23, 42,
    52, 55, 100, 105, 108, 110,
    113, 118, 134, 136, 141,
    152, 158, 164;* people 51–
    3, 123; *and see* Turkey
animistic beliefs 44, 45
Arabs 57, 58, 60
Ardabil 59
Armenia 52, 56; people 51,
    57; *13*
Aryan 51, 62
Asia 32, 34, 51, 58
Asia Minor 32, 51, 52
Assyrians 51
Aubusson 55
Avars 57
Aydin 54; *71, 143*
Azerbaijan 56
Baghdad 52
bags 12, 27, 35, 41, 44, 50, 57,
    60, 123, 125, 147; *62, 81,
    125, 132, 138, 145, 150,
    163;* donkey 28, 50, 147;
    164, 166; and see hurgin;
    saddle 27, 28, 37, 50, 62,
    149; *147, 178;* salt 15, 50,
    125, 147; *147, 178; and see*
    namek donneh; storage
    15, 29, 41, 50, 61, 62, 147;
    142; and see jaloor; juval;
    torbah
Bakhtiari 38, 60, 93; *20, 58,
    79, 128, 142, 150*
balanced plainweave 37, 40;
    37, 86

Balikesir 53–4; *70, 158*
Balouch: kilim 35, 39, 41, 49,
    62; *49, 62, 80, 86, 98, 99,
    102, 105, 108, 114, 118,
    136;* people 28, 30, 32, 34,
    36, 60, 62
Balouchistan 28, 29, 62; *58,
    61*
bathroom 93–4; *114, 116*
bedroom 93; *18, 19, 23, 93,
    106, 113, 114, 116*
Bergama 53–4; *70, 118*
Bessarabia 55; *74*
betrothal *see* dowry;
    marriage
Bijar 59; *76*
border 64, 91, 95; *26, 52, 59,
    60, 62, 73*
boteh 48, 59, 60; *76, 79*
Brahuis 62
brocade 29, 60; *and see* cicim;
    soumak; zilli
bsath 11; *and see* kilim
Bulgaria 52, 53
buying 171–2
Caliph 48
camel 28, 46, 50, 150; *68;*
    hair 30, 32, 49, 93
Canakkale 41
caravan routes *see* trade
    routes
carding 29–30
carpet gripper 126; *132; and
    see* wall hanging
Caspian Sea 62
Cathay 61
Caucasus 12, 28, 29, 41, 56–
    7, 58, 59, 60; *56;* kilim 31,
    37, 41, 50, 56–7; *15, 79,
    116*
Chahar Aimaq 62, 63
Charchaghan 63
chemical fading 53
China 32
Christian 45, 51
cicim 37, 40, 41, 45, 54; *22,
    40, 72, 86*
cleaning 90, 95, 96, 126, 151,
    173–4; *132, 157; and see*
    wear and tear
collecting 170–3
collector 34, 44, 62
colour 27, 31, 32, 33, 34, 36,
    37, 38, 39, 44, 53, 58, 59,
    60, 63, 64, 92, 93, 94, 95,
    96, 147; *and see* dyes
connoisseur 33, 44, 53, 57

conservatory 94; *118*
contour band 38; *38, 73*
corridor 125
cotton 28, 29, 30, 53, 59, 60,
    62, 93
Crimea 52
curtain 40, 149; *19*
curved weft 39; *39*
cushion 147, 149, 151; *145,
    155, 161, 163, 164, 166,
    169*
damp 93, 94, 124, 126
Danube 51
Dasht-i-Margo 62
desert 29, 32, 62
dining room 94, 96; *23, 96,
    110*
donkey 50; *68*
Dost Mohammed 62
double interlock tapestry
    38, 39, 60, 64, 93; *38, 79,
    86*
dovetailing 38, 39, 63, 64; *38,
    84, 86*
dowry 13, 29, 36, 48, 94; *and
    see* marriage
drawing room *see* living
    room
durability *see* wear and tear
dyeing: ingredients 31–4;
    techniques 31–4
dyer 31–3
dyes, chemical 16, 31–4, 57,
    62, 64, 92, 124, 170, 173,
    174; *66, 164;* natural 12,
    16, 27, 31–4, 53, 59, 62,
    92, 124, 170, 173, 174; *65,
    110*
eating cloth *see* soffrai
elibelinde 46; *46*
Ertugrul 52
Erzurum 55; *74*
evil eye *see* nazarlik
export 16, 171
extra weft insets 39, 59; *39*
Ezari 63
Fars 60; *99*
Farsi 62
Fatima 48
felt 49, 64; *and see* namad;
    underfelt
field 40, 45, 54, 95; *26*
First Crusade 52
flatweave *see* kilim; weaving
floor surface 90, 91, 93, 94,
    95, 96; *106, 113, 114, 178,
    184*

flower *see* gul
folk art 44, 63
folk tale 45
France 55
fringe 39, 126; *26, 82*
furnishing 40, 149, 151
Garmsar 15, 60; *23, 77, 113,
    163, 164*
gelim 11; *and see* kilim
Georgia 56, 57
Ghazni 61, 63
Ghengis Khan 64
Ghilzai sheep 62
Ghor 63
ghujeri 40, 64, 149; *66, 85,
    87, 106, 110, 118, 158*
goat 12, 27, 28, 46, 62; *65;*
    hair 30, 32, 54, 93
gol 46
Golden Fleece, The 28
Greece 53, 61
Greeks, the 51, 56, 58
guard band 39; *26*
gul 46, 55, 61, 63, 64; *47, 74,
    83, 85*
Hali 172, 173
hallway 94–5; *19, 89, 94, 95,
    96, 99, 128, 141, 180*
hand-on-hip motif *see*
    elibelinde
hanging kilims *see* wall
    hanging
Hazara 62, 64
Herat 62, 63; *68*
Herati pattern 59; *76*
Hindu Kush 64
Holtzer, Ernst 11, 13, 15
horse 12, 28, 149, 150; cover
    60, 150; *77*
Hungary 52
Huns 51
hurgin 50, 147, 148; *130, 148,
    164; and see* bags
Iliad 12
India 12, 61, 62
indigo 31, 32, 63; *and see* dyes
Indonesia 11
Indus 31
insulation 123, 125, 151; *145*
interior designer 16, 90, 94;
    136
investment 170–3
Iraq 51, 56
Iran 16, 51, 63, 171; *and see*
    Persia
Islam 44, 45, 46, 48, 52
Islamic art 27, 44, 45

Istanbul 171
jaloor 15, 50, 61, 147, 149,
    150; *50; and see* bags
Jason 27
jewelry 12, 13
juval 15, 41, 50, 61, 147; *and
    see* bags
Kagizman 42
Kandahar 62, 63
Karabagh 55; *74*
Kara Kum desert 63
Karaman 54
Karaqul sheep 62, 63
Kars 56; *75*
Kayseri 54–5; *73*
Kazakh 64; *61, 85, 143, 157*
Kettles Yard, Cambridge *141*
Khoorjeen *see* hurgin
Khorasan 48, 50, 60–1
Kilil Kum desert 64
kilim: antique 16, 53, 54, 93,
    123, 170, 171; *110, 134,
    141, 143, 176;*
    commercial 53, 57, 170;
    composition 44, 57, 60,
    91, 95, 123, 124; court 28,
    52; floral 45, 46, 52, 53,
    55, 58, 59, 95; *74, 76, 77,
    136, 157;* halves 54, 55,
    56, 62; *71, 73, 74, 80, 163;*
    history 11, 12–16, 28–9,
    31, 51–3, 57, 58, 59, 90,
    123; modern 16, 48, 53,
    55, 63, 93, 170; *74, 113,
    136;* nomadic 15, 52, 53,
    57, 60, 62; *143, 166;*
    reversible 38, 125, 151;
    161; traditional use 12,
    15, 16, 29, 58, 90, 123,
    151; *65, 66, 68, 155;*
    village 15, 53; *76, 128;*
    Western influence 46–8,
    53, 59, 63, 90; workshop
    15, 28, 52, 53, 57, 58, 59,
    170; *71, 76, 143*
Kirghiz 30; *66*
kitchen 96, 125; *23, 24, 96,
    118, 157, 158, 182*
knotted carpet 11, 12, 33, 36,
    37, 45, 46, 48, 49, 57, 63,
    152, 174; *81, 136*
Konya 41, 52, 54, 93; *54, 68,
    71*
Kuba 57; *56, 75, 178*
Kurdish kilim 48, 49, 51; *16,
    60, 74, 75, 136*
Kurdistan 51, 58, 59; *58*

Kurds 30, 34, 51, 55, 56, 57, 58, 59, 60; *73*
kylym 11; *and see* kilim
Labijar 63; *83, 118, 164*
Lakai 64; *85, 143; and see* Kazakh
lake *see* gol
lanolin 29, 174
'lazy lines' 37, 39; *74*
lighting: artificial 62, 92, 93, 95, 124; *125, 134, 138;* natural 62, 92, 94, 95, 124; *98, 116, 125, 128, 143*
living room 94, 95; *20, 91, 95, 100, 102, 106, 110, 116*
loom 12, 27, 34, 37, 38, 57; ground 34, 53, 60, 62, 63; *11,35, 66, 82, 163;* vertical 34, 53, 64; *and see* weaving
Lurs 60
madder 32, 49, 63; *83, 85, 132; and see* dyes
maffrash 50, 149; *and see* bags
Maimana 63, 64; *64, 84, 100, 105, 106, 110, 163*
Malatya 55; *73, 138, 142, 157, 182*
Manastir 54; *70*
marriage 13, 15, 36, 150; *and see* dowry
Mashed 62
meal cloth *see* soffrai
Mecca 48
medallion 45, 54, 55, 57, 59; *9, 54, 75, 77*
Middle East 44
mihrab 48, 49, 54, 55, 59, 123; *72, 74, 81, 136, 138; and see* prayer rug
Mogul 61
Mohammed 48
Mongol 51, 52, 58, 64
mordant 31, 32; *132; and see* dyes
mosque 12, 48, 49, 54, 123; *68*
moth 126
motif 12, 16, 44–8, 53, 57, 59, 60, 63, 64, 92, 124; *45, 46, 47, 48, 77, 79, 82, 83, 84; and see* symbols
Mughan 59
Mukkur 63; *82, 96*
Muslim 48; Shi'ah 64; Sunni 63
Mut 41, 54; *71, 86*
namad 15; *and see* felt

namek donneh 50; *and see* salt bags
nazarlik 48; *48*
nomads 13, 27, 32, 33, 34, 36, 50, 51, 60, 62, 147, 149; *65, 68;* semi- 32, 52, 56, 57, 62, 63; *65, 68*
Novatreat 173
Nuristan *131*
Obruk 52, 54; *72*
office 125; *106*
Oriental Rug Review, The 172, 173
Ottoman: empire 52, 53, 123; people 52, 56
Pahari 58, 60
palas 11; *and see* kilim
Palestine 52
parpak 15; *and see* tent band
Parsons, W. D. 15
Parthian 61
Pashtun 62, 63
pattern 27, 44, 47, 51, 53, 58, 62, 63, 92, 93, 94, 95, 96, 124, 125, 147
Perkin, W. H. 33
Persia 12, 15, 16, 28, 29, 38, 39, 40, 49, 62, 63, 123; *58;* kilim 15, 28, 29, 35, 38, 39, 40, 46, 58–61; *11, 12, 22, 24, 59, 106, 110, 180, 182;* people 30, 47, 57, 58–9; *11; and see* Iran
Phoenicians 31
plainweave *see* balanced plainweave
playroom 96; *113*
prayer rug 35, 44, 48, 49, 54, 56, 59, 93, 123; *20, 23, 55, 72, 74, 75, 105, 113, 125, 136, 138; and see* mihrab
prayers 48
proverb 28
Punjab 62
purdah 15, 123
Qala-i-Nau 39, 63; *81*
Qashqai 29, 30, 34, 59, 60; *58, 79, 108, 143, 161, 166*
Qazvin 59; *113*
Quetta 62
Qur'an 44, 45, 147
Rajasthan 19, 157
Red Sea 52
repairs 174; *184*
Rezah Shah 58
room divider 125, 151, *161*
rope 28, 40, 149; *68*

Rukhshanis 62
rukorsi 49, 150; *49, 114; and see* soffrai
runner 49, 55, 59, 63, 64, 90, 91, 93, 94, 95, 147, 149; *23, 77, 79, 82, 91, 98, 99, 102, 114, 118*
Ruskin, John 31
Russia 56, 57, 59, 61, 62, 63
Russian Revolution 57
'S' Twist 30; *31; and see* spinning
saf 49, 54; *100; and see* mihrab
Safavid 29, 58, 59, 123
Salor 63; *and see* Turkoman
Samurs 57
Sandanaj 59; *and see* Senna
Sar-i-Pul 63, 64; *84*
Sarkoy 53; *163*
Sarmayie 39, 63; *82, 106*
Sassanian 58, 61
Sava 59
Savonnerie 55
scorpion 46, 48; *46, 57; and see* motif
seat 148, 149, 150, 151–2; *142, 163, 166*
Seljuk Turks 52, 59; *and see* Turks
selling 173
selvedge 28, 63, 90, 126, 174; *26*
Senna 28, 35, 36, 58; *19, 76, 108, 132, 143*
Shahsavan 59, 60; *58, 77, 142*
Shamanistic belief 44
sheep 12, 27, 28, 29, 46, 62, 63, 64, 93; *65*
Shemakha 41
Shirvan 51; *56, 75*
silk 29, 30
Sind 62
single interlock tapestry *see* dovetailing
Sirrihisar 41
Sivas 55; *73, 121, 134*
slitweave 37, 45, 47, 54, 57, 59, 60, 63, 64, 92, 93, 95; *37, 71, 73, 77, 82, 84*
snake 46
soapwort 174
sofa *see* seat
soffrai 49, 93, 150; *18, 49, 80, 114, 155, 157, 161*
soumak 40, 41, 45, 59, 60, 62, 63, 93; *41, 77, 79, 80, 81, 85, 86*

spider 46, 48, 64; *46, 57, 85; and see* motif
spinning 29, 30–1; machine 31, 53; techniques 30; tools 30; *30*
stains *see* cleaning
stairs *19, 163*
studio *100*
study 94; *100, 125, 182*
Suleyman II 52
Suleyman Shah 52
sun fading 53
Swarfega 174
Swat *131*
symbol 44–8, 52, 64; *and see* motif
Syria *66*
taboo 45
Taimani 63; *61, 81*
tapestry, European 45, 55
tapestry weave *see* weft-face weave
Tartari 64; *19, 61, 85, 86, 89*
Tartars 56
Taurus mountains 54
Tehran 60
Tekke 29, 61, 63; *and see* Turkoman
tent 12, 28, 36, 123, 125, 148, 151; *and see* yurt
tent band 28, 40, 147, 149; *66, 68, 166; and see* parpak
texture 27, 35, 92, 93, 96, 124, 147
Third Crusade 52
Thrace 38, 52, 53; *70, 74, 131, 141*
Timurlaine 52
torbah 15; *and see* bags
tourist 16, 53, 56, 171
trade route 44, 51, 56, 60, 61, 62
Tree of Life 48; *131, 132; and see* motif
tribal: folklore 44; movement 15, 16,51, 52, 56–7
tribes 27, 44, 51, 52, 53, 56, 57, 58, 60, 61, 62, 63, 64, 93
Tugrul Bey, Sultan 52
Turkestan 28, 38, 50; *61*
Turkey 15, 16, 38, 40, 41, 51, 171; *68; and see* Anatolia
Turkoman: kilim 47, 50, 63; *83;* people 29, 51, 58, 60, 61, 62, 63

Turks 51, 52, 56, 57
underlay 90–1, 92, 93, 95, 96; *89, 118, 184*
Usak 52; *113*
Uzbek 60, 63, 64; *85, 87, 106, 110, 118, 158*
valuation 172–3
Van 29, 30, 52, 56; *75*
Veramin 60; *77*
wall hanging 124, 126–8; *121, 125, 132, 134, 138, 141, 163;* surface 123, 124
warp 28, 34, 35, 37, 38, 39, 40, 53, 54, 56, 60, 62, 126; *26, 66*
warp-face patterning 40, 64; *40, 85, 87*
water rights 13, 29
washing kilims 173–4; *and see* cleaning
wear and tear 90, 92, 93, 94, 95, 96, 151, 173–4; *89*
weaver 33, 35, 36, 37, 38, 45, 47, 48, 51, 53, 55, 170; *66*
weaving 16, 36, 37, 38, 39, 40, 62; *26, 66;* history 12, 27; techniques 12, 36–41, 124; *26, 66;* tools 36
weft 35, 37, 38, 39, 40, 59, 60, 62, 126; *26*
weft-face patterning 39, 40, 45, 60, 62, 63; *39, 80, 82, 86*
weft-face weave 37, 50, 54; *37, 81*
weft wrapping 41, 60; *73*
wool 12, 27, 28, 29, 30, 32, 33, 34, 36, 44, 53, 54, 55, 56, 57, 59, 60, 62, 63, 64, 124; *66;* washing 29; shearing 29; *and see* carding; spinning
yarn 31, 32, 35, 39, 40, 53, 55, 57, 59, 60, 92, 93, 149; *and see* cotton; silk; wool
Yomut 29, 61, 63; *and see* Turkoman
Yoruk 51, 52, 53, 54
yurt 50, 64, 149; *68; and see* tent